SEXUAL ISSUES IN SOCIAL WORK

Steve Myers and Judith Milner

Consultant editor: Jo Campling

BASW

BRITISH ASSOCIATION
OF SOCIAL WORKERS

First published in Great Britain in 2007 by

The Policy Press
University of Bristol
Fourth Floor
Beacon House
Queen's Road
Bristol BS8 1QU
UK

Tel +44 (0)117 331 4054
Fax +44 (0)117 331 4093
e-mail tpp-info@bristol.ac.uk
www.policypress.org.uk

British Library Cataloguing in Publication Data
A catalogue record for this book is available from the British Library.

Library of Congress Cataloging-in-Publication Data
A catalog record for this book has been requested.

ISBN 978 1 86134 712 1 paperback
ISBN 978 1 86134 713 8 hardcover

Cover design by Qube Design Associates, Bristol.
Front cover: photograph supplied by kind permission of Getty Images.
Printed and bound in Great Britain by MPG Books, Bodmin.

In memory of Jo Campling, an inspiration always.
Forever grateful.

Contents

List of figures

Introduction

This book has its origins in the interest of both authors in sex through their engagement with professional (and, of course, personal) issues raised primarily within social work. Judith Milner wrote *Social Work and Sexual Problems* (1986) at a time when such a topic was subjected to political, moral, medical and legal arguments that tended to obscure rather than illuminate the necessity for social workers to think about sex as an influence on their practice, leading to categorisation, assumption and (equally as problematic) certainty about the nature and role of sex within social work. As practitioners in social work and counselling, the authors have frequently been faced with matters of sex that raise their heads in the most unusual and often unexpected ways, often addressed through unhelpful and damaging practices that serve to reinforce the oppression of the very people they are supposed to be assisting. Sex has generally been considered within social work through 'problem' sex, including lesbian and gay sexualities, sexual health, sexual offending or misbehaviours, under-age sexuality, sexual victimisation, sex working and so on. There has been a move towards promoting healthy sexuality and an increasing recognition that sex is a central part of people's lived experience and also a right, with sexual expression a matter to be included in assessment and intervention in people's lives.

Both of the authors have experience of including sex within teaching in social work training and education; of direct work with people who have 'problem' sex, be they victims or perpetrators of sexual aggression; of training social workers in ways of thinking of and approaching sexual behaviours; and of questioning the often prejudicial attitudes and behaviours of those they have worked with. This has helped them to recognise that sex can be a powerful and visceral topic that can generate strong feelings that then inform working assumptions and influence practice in ways that are not always helpful. Examples the authors have come across in their work include: an experienced and avowedly feminist child protection worker saying in a training session that 'boys just want sex and girls just want chocolates'; during a workshop on HIV, one member disclosing his HIV positive status and another member saying that they were not surprised given who he was (an 'out' gay man); a senior social worker explaining to a white boy in foster care that "we did not hold hands with other men in the street, that is something Asian men do"; women service users being condemned for taking yet another unsuitable male partner; an eight-year-old boy being described as a 'mini-perp' for his inappropriate sexual behaviours; and a judge sentencing a rapist to a shorter sentence than that available because his 15-year-old male victim was 'soiled goods', having been involved in prostitution.

The above examples begin to indicate that sex and sexualities are rather complicated, with a variety of different discourses, labels and identities influencing the sense people make of sexual matters. Gender, race, ability, age, sexual orientation, fertility and health – and readers may want to add to these categories – all cross and interact with sex and sexuality. This can make social work practice very complicated, or at least it should do. The lack of discussion, or, more accurately, the *ways* in which sex is discussed and conceptualised, may lead to assumptions that have unhelpful consequences for service users. For example, in one case in the authors' experience, a girl subjected to a single sexual assault by a peer acquaintance was assumed to require 'counselling' due to the traumatic nature of the event. She was referred to a group for girls who had been sexually abused, yet left after one session because the rest of the group had been systematically abused by members of their families over a long period of time, an experience she could not relate to. Nor did the therapy address her specific needs. Questions were asked about her denial as she had been subsumed into the category 'abused' without any sense of the complexity and individuality of her own experience. She had been constructed as a victim, which became her identity with all the expectations of this. The good intentions of the referrers had been influenced by assumptions about the nature of sexual abuse. It is difficult to be clear about the meanings and effects of sexual abuses when there is no one sexuality. Moreover, the authors have frequently come across cases where young people have been described as being 'confused about their sexuality'. Although this sounds neutral enough, it never seems to mean that a young person doubts that they are gay and considers that they may be heterosexual; it is a code for thinking about being gay. It is probably better to be clearer about what we are saying rather than to perpetuate talk that continues to obscure. More than anything, it is important to ask people what their understandings of sex and sexuality are.

The book uses terms that are common yet contested and aims to explore how language can influence and define thinking about sex and sexualities. The ways in which sex has been conceptualised are explored, particularly academic developments in understanding and explaining this phenomenon. The intention is to offer practical ways of working with sex and sexuality. The selection of material in this book is to some extent artificial, yet it provides some thematic structure. The authors use a selection of their own practice scenarios, although readers may prefer to substitute their own. Readers may exercise their judgement by identifying specific topics that are of practice interest, or may well find that their case examples cross these boundaries. Given the all-pervasiveness of sex and sexuality, it is probable that there will be overlaps, commonalities and some repetition. The authors consider this to be inevitable but have attempted to provide at least some material for thought.

This book is also more than simply a 'how to work with' text, although that is part of its function, because the authors take the view that there are difficulties in compartmentalising people and confining their rich individuality to the label they have been given, usually by someone in a position of power. Suppose you wanted to write about heterosexual men. How could you begin to capture the variety of individuals who inhabit this label? Are they all the same all of the time? What would be their commonalities apart from a broad sexual interest in women? You might choose to look at the specific problems faced by heterosexual men who spend vast amounts of energy conforming to a macho stereotype, when in actual fact they struggle to fit this role.

Throughout this book, the authors do not use these terms unambiguously, but in ways that they hope will allow for reflection on the context in which they are used and the ways in which we make assumptions through using specific language and concepts. The way we think and talk about sex and sexuality will lead to social work actions and practices that have consequences for those subjected to them. Consider the following example:

Janine was concerned that her four-year-old son Peter was spending too much time with herself, her sisters and her daughters and too little time with other boys and Peter's estranged father. She was anxious that being in a predominantly female environment would 'affect his sexuality'.

What are the expectations of gender within this example? What is being said and what is left unsaid about how sexuality is created and thought of? How as a social care worker would you assist Janine in reducing her anxiety? To what extent do you share Janine's concerns? How do you think this could 'affect his sexuality'? What normative judgements are being made within the example?

To be helpful to busy social care workers, the book aims to outline some of the key concepts and debates within sex and sexuality in ways that do not presume too much about prior reading or assume that people should have read or understood some of the contemporary knowledge issues. The authors' experience of talking about sex in practice and education has led them to believe that a straightforward approach is the best for everyone, even where this may lead to offence to some, embarrassment for others and humour for many. Sex is spoken of in many different ways in our society, but often in codes and metaphors and in rather formulaic and emotionally powerful ways. As Wilton (2004, p 1) says:

> Sex is a challenging subject to communicate about. Policed by social and cultural taboo, complicated by psychological, emotional and existential significance ... it is easy to say the wrong thing about sex.

Bearing this in mind, the authors attempt to provide basic information and pointers for further reading as some of the debates raised are fluid and change rapidly, depending on the prevailing thoughts, research and social morality of the time.

Part One
Making sense of sex and sexuality

This section describes the theories that have influenced social policies and practices. It then outlines more contemporary theories that question more traditional understandings. Some of these theories are taught on social work courses, some have become part of popular psychologies; therefore, social workers' understandings of sex and sexuality will have emerged from a mixture of both and, of course, from their own experiences. Readers are invited to locate the roots of their understanding in the various explanations introduced in this part of the book. Chapter One looks at traditional explanations rooted in physiology and psychiatry. Chapter Two examines how these explanations are moderated by social factors and how the meanings of sex and sexuality do not remain fixed. Chapter Three outlines some of the ways in which social policies regulate sex and sexuality, including some of the legislation and guidance that set the parameters of social work practice.

ONE

Sex, sexuality and the body

As we use language to describe and make sense of the world, it is useful to start by outlining some of the meanings attached to our use of the terms 'sex' and 'sexualities'. There is room for confusion here, as the terms can have slightly (or greatly) different meanings depending on who is using them, where, when and how. So sex may mean the biological gender of a person or sexual activities. Often when completing forms or surveys, a question will be asked about your sex, meaning whether you are male or female. Yet a sex survey in a popular magazine will probably be more interested in the sexual attitudes and activities of readers. Sexuality tends to mean the sexual attitudes, expressions and practices of the person, yet this can also have different boundaries drawn around it (Saraga, 1998). It can be a category ('What is his sexuality? He is gay'), or an action ('She is expressing her sexuality'). It can be limited to specific sexual activities, or broadened to include many aspects of a person's life including fertility, dress and friendships.

Within this range of meanings there are some (often obscured) value judgements made about sex and sexualities. Not least is the idea that there are norms of sex and sexuality that are the preferred and privileged ways of being in our society, leading to assumptions about people that can be unhelpful. The idea that people have a fixed sexuality, for example, is very strong, with particular performances attached to these. Consider the notion of our heterosexual man. What does this mean? We know that it has some indication of sexual preference, yet this seems unlikely to be the whole story. The identity of heterosexuality means significantly more than simply genital sexual choice; it comes with other meanings (and expectations) attached to it. How men behave in a heterosexual way can include ambivalence about women, expectations of gender roles, notions of what it is to be a father, fear of being seen to be effeminate, economic expectations and so on. These are more than just natural; they are formed and performed within our society and have a clear (if somewhat fragile) set of rules around them. The concept of heterosexuality also pervades social structures, including welfare provision and the delivery of services that are often based on the man and woman in marriage/partnership. More than this, heterosexuality is seen as the norm against which people in their diversity are measured, with other sexualities losing out as being unnatural or deficient in the face of the taken-for-granted assumptions of heterosexuality. Yet the privileges accorded to heterosexuality come at a price, with severe restrictions on how people are allowed to think and behave. The boundaries of heterosexuality have to be policed and reinforced through social interactions; otherwise it may well collapse. This rigidity can be uncomfortable for those who find that they have aspects of their behaviour or feelings that do not conform to the narrow range permissible within this way of thinking. As social care workers are continually making moral judgements about others, it is important to explore how social work(ers) may consciously or unconsciously reinforce these ways of thinking, thus enabling a more thoughtful practice to emerge.

Sexual behaviours

Sexual behaviour encompasses a vast range of actions, some of which are fairly common and shared by a great many people, while others are less universally accepted or enjoyed. In many ways, sexual behaviours are a matter of personal taste, in that there is a variety of acts that can be performed: alone, with another, with others or with objects. Some are intellectual, while others may be physical. These behaviours have a long history varied with the advent of social and technological change. For example, the viewing of visual and textual pornography has been influenced by printing, film, video and the internet, giving opportunities that were not previously available (and in the process creating opportunities for broadening abusive sexual behaviours). Defining what are normal sexual behaviours becomes problematic when faced with this range of actions, as they are limited only by imagination and the physical body (although cyberspace presents some challenges even to these limits). Sexual behaviours are regulated by social and cultural forces, encouraging some and abhorring others, defining what can be done, with whom, with which parts of the body and when (Plummer, 1984). In one training programme run by the authors, one of the participants had an extreme reaction to the very idea of anal sex, which went beyond the bounds of a moral distaste. When gently asked to share her concerns, it emerged that she was under the (mistaken) impression that such an act could physically traumatise the body and lead to heart seizure. Genuine in her concerns, she had not had the opportunity to discuss this previously due to taboos on what was acceptable social conversation.

Trying to gain some understanding of what sexual behaviours people actually *do* is in itself a problematic task. Imagine being approached to take part in a survey about your preferred sexual practices. What would you feel comfortable about disclosing? What level of confidentiality would you require about the answers? Would you prefer a checklist of behaviours to tick, or would you prefer to describe them in your own words? The research on sexual behaviour is understandably limited by these and other considerations, heavily influenced by what people feel they should say about this morally contentious area. Researching sexual fantasies is another aspect of sexuality that is dependent on the honesty and ability of people to discuss what they feel, and any claims to understanding fantasies must be moderated as a result.

If it is difficult to say what is normal, it may be possible to say what exists and what may be more common in frequency of occurrence and across the population. We can also then accept that some things are less common, without viewing this as necessarily abnormal. Sex surveys abound in popular magazines, although they tend to give limited insight into behaviours, but perhaps only marginally less than other more scientific studies. The work of Kinsey et al (1948) is often cited as a key development in the understanding of sexual behaviour, in that it featured a large study of men and their sexual habits, experiences and views. This led to some startling (for then, but perhaps also now) findings, which included that a large minority of his subjects admitted to some same-sex sexual behaviours that had led to orgasm. This led to serious moral outrage and concern that the morals of the United States (where the study was undertaken) were at risk, resulting in political campaigns and possibly influencing a legal clampdown on same-sex behaviours. Of course, the study has since been criticised for a number of methodological flaws (one being that it may have been undertaken in a gay area), but the difficulty of researching this field is clearly outlined; this is a terrain fraught with political-moral debates and disagreements. Claims and counterclaims about, for example, the number of lesbians and gay men in the population are based on notions that you can identify such categories of people, a difficult definitional problem as we have seen previously, let alone telling us little about their sexual behaviours.

Make a list of all the sexual behaviours you consider to be heterosexual. Now make a list of all those sexual behaviours you consider to be homosexual. Which sexual actions can *only* be performed by heterosexuals and which *only* by homosexuals?

Even behaviour that we disapprove of for the very good reason that it is abusive and causes harm to others does not necessarily have to be abnormal; it is merely crossing a moral line that we consider to be unacceptable. In the UK, a married woman could not bring a legal charge of rape against her husband until the early 1990s. The violence of rape had a different meaning within the institution of marriage in previous years, linked to notions of the submission of women and their status as possessions of their husbands.

So, sexual behaviours are difficult to categorise as ab/normal, but we can explore what is known about their frequency. The sexual behaviour of children generates a great deal of anxiety and we have seen professionals and parents extremely concerned about making sense of their children's behaviours. Research has been undertaken to uncover what children do at different ages and how these may be viewed as expected or normal. Freudian theoretical approaches provide a developmental model of childhood sexuality, but there is also some empirical evidence about what children do. However, this is an area littered with personal moral and cultural influences, so you are invited to complete the following exercise before exploring some of the evidence.

Which sexual behaviours would you expect in children of the following ages?	
Age	**Sexual behaviour**
0–2	
3–4	
5–8	
9–13	
14–16	
17–18	

This exercise raises a definitional problem of what constitutes 'sexual' with children. How have you defined sexual? What is the relationship with 'sensual'? It has been found in teaching and training that people struggle with defining younger children's behaviour as sexual, but can apply this to older age groups. However, it has also been found that although many participants take a fairly liberal approach to expected sexual activity for young teenagers, this does not mean that they think that this is appropriate or desirable for their own children. It can be helpful to complete this exercise independently and then compare it with another person's list in order to gain some understanding of the similarities and differences of opinion about this area. Due to the lack of empirical evidence and social reluctance to discuss such matters, many people draw on their own personal experiences to inform their construction of childhood sexual behaviours. This can have the consequence of encouraging a narrow and personal view of sexual behaviours that is unhelpful to others.

In defining what is sexual, we have to recognise that behaviour in younger children that would be sexual if they were adults does not have the same meaning for them. So infants often stimulate their own genitals and baby boys can have erections, but this does not relate directly to adult sexual behaviour, and their understanding of the behaviour is different (Chaffin et al, 2002). This is important in the current climate of concern about sexual abuse and how we may unwittingly categorise children's behaviour as abusive as if it were the same as adult behaviour. Friedrich et al (1998) undertook a large study (1,114 children between the ages of two and 12) of childhood sexual behaviours reported by mothers in the US and found the following in more than 10% of the sample:

- standing too close to people;
- touching sexual parts in public;
- masturbating with their hand;
- touching breasts;
- touching their sexual parts at home;
- trying to look at people when they are naked;
- showing sexual parts to adults;
- hugging adults not well known to them;
- being very interested in the opposite sex.

There were differences in frequency of behaviour depending on the age of the child, with younger children much more likely to engage in the above behaviours than older children, and although there were some differences between boys and girls, these were not hugely significant. Many of the described behaviours were dependent on the interpretation of the mothers and the researchers, which, as we have seen with the exercise, can lead to different understandings of the same actions. It is also dependent on mothers being able to recognise the behaviour, which is by its nature often hidden from view, as well as being culturally defined within the context of the US. Hackett (2004) helpfully outlines some of the debates about the differences between expected and concerning sexual behaviours in children, including a definition from Chaffin et al (2002) that identifies behaviours that may be of concern:

- occurs at a frequency greater than would be developmentally expected;
- interferes with the child's development;
- occurs with coercion, intimidation or force;
- is associated with emotional distress;
- occurs between children of divergent ages or developmental abilities;
- repeatedly recurs in secrecy after intervention by caregivers (Hackett, 2004, p 88).

This assists in making sense of the range of behaviours exhibited by children, allowing us to begin to differentiate between expected and potentially problematic actions.

The essential biology of sex

One of the key elements of discussions about sex is the tension of the nature–nurture debate, whereby people argue that sex can be something that is an *essential* biological fact, inherent in our human make-up, or something that is tempered or created through social experience and conditioning. These arguments are often played out within gender (in itself a contested concept, to be explored later), where individuals, families, cultures and legal systems have certain expectations of the supposed male and female roles, with claims supported by the evidence of science, biology and the idea of naturalness. The biological imperative for sex is often marshalled in terms of reproduction of the species, promotion of individual (and group) gene pools, or sex drive, all of which are seen as underpinning sexual behaviour. There is little doubt that sexual feelings exist; however, ideas of where these come from are usually linked to theoretical or moral concepts about normality. Thus a biological determinist (one who believes in the absolute centrality of the biological imperative to sex) may use this notion to claim specific roles for men and women in their sexual behaviour because it is *natural*. If sexual feelings and expression are socially influenced, then the environment in which children are raised will be of prime importance and should be scrutinised to ensure that they have a healthy sexuality. Both social and biological arguments can lead to an enforcement of sexual norms despite having different roots. This chapter now outlines some of the key essentialist understandings of sex and sexuality and how these may influence our work with people.

Sociobiology

Expectations of gender can be supported by claims made by science, for example through sociobiological theoretical perspectives, that view people in society today as the product of evolutionary processes and draw heavily on ideas based on Darwinian notions. Sociobiology can be seen as '... the systematic study of the biological basis of all social behaviour ...' (Wilson, 1975, p 4). Historically, humanity has developed from hunter–gatherer communities and the biological programming required for survival in this environment influences how people behave in contemporary society. From this image of the past, men are seen as hunters and women as nurturers, with associated biological traits such as aggression and sexual predation for men and passivity and homemaking for women. Going out and hunting for food can be transposed as going to work and getting paid – the breadwinner. These ideas can be used to reinforce gendered roles and in particular can be used to explain and excuse the poor behaviour of men and lock women into a particular subservient role. Taylor (1997) has outlined some of the key arguments of these approaches and found that many of the claims are based on a biased reading of the evidence and reflect a speculative view of how early societies functioned based on the dominant norms of those undertaking the analysis. The archaeological example of a body found in a grave with a long implement is cited as an indicative case. The body was originally thought to be male and the implement was called a 'sword'. Later, when the body was proved to be female, the implement was changed into a 'stick'. The gendered expectations of those who have the power to name something are reflected in this example. Such scientific evidence supporting gendered behaviours has consequences; for example, the authors have worked with men who sexually offend who have cited such evidence as explanations (and therefore excuses) for their aggressive behaviour. On a less extreme note, these essentialist explanations for human sexuality are used to support the idea that men are naturally more sexually driven (usually to maximise their genetic legacy or some such reason) than women, who are more concerned about child rearing and stability.

Sociobiology has its basis in ideas of natural selection and the heredity of genes, taking biological understandings of sex as the fundamental explanation for all sexual behaviours. Claims that specific genes have been discovered that have a direct link to particular behaviours are widespread and are used to provide explanations for almost every human action. However, as Nelkin and Lindee (1995, p 388) point out:

> The power of the gene as a cultural icon reflects the appeal of scientific explanations that reinforce and legitimate existing social categories ... sociobiology [has] provided a language through which group differences that are culturally desirable [to the majority] can be interpreted as biologically determined.

In our society, we privilege science to the extent that to state that something is 'scientifically proven' is often enough to end any debate, yet this ignores the contested nature of science and what constitutes evidence. Social assumptions about sex and sexuality can be masked by claims to scientific truth and can have consequences for how this discovery of sex is used.

Scruton (1986), for example, claimed that men need to be tamed through a monogamous marriage to ensure that their rampant, biologically driven sexuality does not create havoc in society. Women's sexuality is seen as passive and focused on domesticity and child rearing. Thus, in this world, women are seen as having the responsibility for managing men's behaviour through providing for their sexual and domestic needs, whatever these may be. The consequences of holding such views are obvious; they place women in a powerless position of responsibility and allow men to blame women for not performing their role effectively when they behave in a sexually irresponsible way. The idea that men have uncontrollable urges and needs (both physical and emotional) reinforces the regulation of women's behaviour, as to be provocative in manner or dress can unleash these primitive male forces, thus leading to sexual attention and/or assault. This rather caveman approach to male sexuality requires women to be alluring to their (married) partners yet demure to other men, allowing men to avoid any sense of personal responsibility or moral reasoning. The idea that sex is a force restrained by a veneer of civilised control, waiting to burst out and wreak havoc, is not new. Weeks (2003, p 17) quotes Malinowski (1963, p 120), who was an anthropologist studying other cultures in the early part of the 20th century, describing sex as:

... a most powerful instinct ... there is no doubt that masculine jealousy, sexual modesty, female coyness, the mechanism of sexual attraction and of courtship – all these forces and conditions made it necessary that even in the most primitive human aggregates there should exist powerful means of regulating, suppressing and directing this instinct.

The idea of sex and sexuality as a force of nature underpins many of the essentialist explanations and can be heard in conversations about sexual processes and practices. Claims by men that once sexual desire is triggered it has to run its course, as if the penis had an independent existence, have been used by sexual offenders known to the authors to explain their aggressive behaviour. Such explanations tend to disappear when it is pointed out that this leaves the offender as a continued danger due to their lack of ability to control themselves, and that the only safe option is permanent incarceration.

James seriously physically assaulted his partner Shaheen after she had an affair with another man. When interviewed, he stated that he was sorry now but that 'any man would have done the same' and that his anger had 'flared up out of control'. He had now 'put a lid on it' and wanted to get back with Shaheen.

What understandings of sex and sexuality are being expressed here? How as a worker with James would you assist him in leading a violence-free life?

Medical bodies

Biomedical understandings of sex and gender have tended to be dominant in Western thinking and these have influenced social work and social care practices. As we know, social work has borrowed heavily from and been influenced by medical ways of understanding the world and this is no different with sex and sexuality. This often surfaces when faced with sexual issues that do not fit the usual expected norm, particularly around same-sex relationships. The idea that there is a normative sexuality called heterosexuality is strong, and this is reinforced by efforts to determine the causality of homosexuality through exploration of, for example, brains (LeVay, 1993), hormones and genes. This approach presumes that there are distinct categories of people that can be labelled heterosexual and homosexual in a biological way, yet there are problems with this and current thinking has questioned whether such distinctions are helpful or true (Weeks, 1985). This will be explored later. Nonetheless, there are continual claims made for the biological basis of all sexual behaviours that take slightly different forms depending on the scientific methods and technologies available at a particular time. The exploration of genes was not possible some years ago but due to changes in science and technology this is an area that can now be investigated and sexuality is an aspect that is subject to this.

Wilton (2000, p 54) identifies two ways in which medical science has tried to explain same-sex desire: hormonal and neurological. In the former, she outlines how it has been theorised that homosexuality has been created through over- or underexposure to male or female hormones, resulting in gay men or lesbian women (Kenen, 1997). Getting the wrong dose or type of hormone sounds plausible and there have been claims that this is supported by experiments with rats (LeVay, 1993). Hormonal explanations have been common but have waned in recent decades, mainly due to the lack of robust scientific evidence to support them (Ruse, 1988). However, they retain some currency and are often used as an explanation for homosexuality in wider society.

The second, neurological, explanation is based on ideas of differences in people's brains, particularly between heterosexual and homosexual people. The work of LeVay (1993, 1996) indicates that there are physical differences in the brains of gay men that seem to have more in common with the brains of heterosexual women than those of heterosexual men. The research was undertaken by investigating the brains of people who had died. However, there are some major problems with the design and analysis of this study that illustrate the ways in which medical science goes about understanding sex and sexuality. First, some of the people had died of AIDS, which can affect the physical structure of the brain. Second, the sexuality of the people was assumed, rather than absolute, and people were assigned a clear hetero-/homosexual category without any thought being given to how complicated such categorisation could be. So, for example, the women investigated were all assumed to be heterosexual, without any consideration that they may well have had other feelings. As they were all dead, they were unable to answer any questions about their sexual preferences, and the information about them came from other sources. Even if they had been in a position to discuss their sexuality, there are very good reasons to believe that they may not have wished to identify their sexual preferences because of the fear of prejudice and discrimination, as well as perhaps not wanting to be categorised in this way. The research of LeVay has been used to support arguments for genetic differences causing sexual preference, but LeVay himself stated that: 'Time and time again I have been described as someone who "proved that homosexuality is genetic" … I did not …' (LeVay, 1996, p 122). He recognised that his study did not provide the robust scientific evidence required to substantiate such a claim, although he seems to have remained convinced that the physical differences he found did have a causal link to sexual preference. Despite extensive exploration of differences, there has been remarkably little hard scientific evidence that demonstrates anything biologically unique about lesbian and gay people as opposed to a notion of the heterosexual, nor is their anything conclusive about the genetic causality of specific sexualities.

Debates about the biological basis of sexual preference continue, with claims made for the differences of lesbian and gay people from a presumed heterosexual norm that have led to interesting arguments about civil rights. If lesbian and gay sexuality is due to biology, then it can be argued to be part of the natural order of things in the same way that heterosexuality is, thereby warranting acceptance and a rejection of being viewed as unnatural. This argument undermines legislation against lesbian and gay people, as many anti-gay laws make claims of defending nature. If the claimed lesbian and gay biology is accepted as a continuum of normalities, rather than a pathological condition that requires correction, then acceptance as part of the range of human expression makes some sense. Thus biological arguments about the nature of difference can be used to support the social acceptance of lesbian and gay people. However, there are potential difficulties with this, not least of which is the possibility of identifying the genetic markers of lesbian and gay foetuses and arguing for termination through prejudice or supposed concern for the quality of the child's life, similar to the use of abortion for female and impaired foetuses in some societies. This has been recognised and has led to some scientists being concerned that '… there is something reductive and scary about a situation in which you might be able to ask a mother whether she wants testosterone treatment to avoid having a gay son' (Allen, 1997, p 242).

Do you believe that a person's sexual preferences are decided biologically or socially? What has led you to believe this? How does this influence you in your work with people?

The psychology of sex and sexuality

Social work education and practice has been heavily influenced by psychological explanations of behaviour (see, for example, Milner and O'Byrne, 2002) and psychology has provided some explanations for and answers to sexual matters. Indeed, lay understandings of sex and sexuality are also heavily influenced by psychological approaches, as any observation of confessional chat shows will demonstrate, with common reference to being in denial, repression, acting out, transference and latency, all terms that have their roots in psychological explanations for behaviour. Psychoanalysis in particular has sex at the centre of all human behaviours and the importance of Freudian ideas in the way we make sense of sexual matters must be acknowledged. Psychoanalysis sees the sex drive, or libido, as the force behind behaviour, either through direct causality or through shaping and influencing expression. Behaviour that may not at first appear to be sexual can be hypothesised within psychoanalysis to have a sexual element or wish, often unconsciously. Thus a psychoanalytically minded social worker may view the illegal entering of a house by a (male) burglar as a sublimated desire to penetrate, or the stealing of a car as the unconscious wish to achieve sexual potency (these are examples from practice that the authors have come across). Such hypotheses will lead to certain practices with the offender, particularly focused on their inner workings and past experiences that require an informed analysis to liberate them from such motivations. Of course, if the person does not accept these explanations but prefers to view their motivations as influenced by social factors such as peer pressure, they may well be understood to be 'in denial', a common defence mechanism within this theoretical framework.

Freudian ideas have a strong normative approach to sexual development and expression, beginning in childhood, emerging through stages and continuing towards the achievement of a complete adult sexuality. A caveat is warranted here, as Freud has been misrepresented or re-emphasised through others in ways that he would probably have found problematic, particularly the tendency of some US psychoanalytical adherents to be simplistic, rigid and absolute about his ideas of what constitutes normality (see, for example, Erikson, 1948; Socarides, 1978). Freud was much more liberal about sexual expressions than many subsequent psychoanalysts, viewing variations from the heterosexual norm as being expected and common, the product of the hugely complex negotiation between the inner and outer worlds during development, and he resisted attempts to condemn homosexuality. However, the very idea of a norm led to ambivalence and contradiction about the range of human sexualities, as variations were inevitably seen as the product of some fault in the psychic process of development. Normative judgements have inevitably been made that led to psychotherapeutic practices that viewed non-heterosexuality as faulty and therefore requiring correction.

Denman (2004) outlines some of the key concepts within Freud relating to sex and sexuality in a clear and thoughtful way. She identifies that Freud first formulated the notion that many adult behavioural difficulties experienced by women were due to early childhood 'seduction', what we would recognise as child sexual abuse, by their fathers. However, he changed his views on this and developed the idea that what his patients were describing were deeply held fantasies of childhood sexual wishes, that they were part of a pattern of normal psychic development rendered unpleasant and damaging by social disapproval and repression. Thus women who claimed that they had been sexually abused in childhood, particularly by their fathers, were dismissed as acting out inner conflicts around childhood development (Masson, 1984). The consequences of this are obvious: women and girls could be disbelieved when they made such claims with a ready-made medical model of explanation. Not only was it difficult for women to be heard in the first place, but such theoretical understandings also located the problem *within them* rather than within those who had abused them and the gendered power structures that enabled this to happen.

Jane alleged that her father was sexually abusing her children as he had abused her when she was a child. The allegations were taken seriously, an investigation was undertaken and her father was charged with serious sexual offences against his grandchildren. Concern was expressed that Jane had not been vigilant in protecting her children, knowing that her father was an abuser (failure to protect).

- *What are your feelings about Jane? To what extent is she responsible for the harm to the children?*

During the investigation, it emerged that 30 years ago when she was 14 Jane had been arrested for breaking a window and taken to Juvenile Court where she alleged that her father was 'being dirty with her'. The court had told Jane not to make up stories to excuse her behaviour and to get her father into trouble. She had been returned to the care of her father.

> • *What are your feelings about Jane? To what extent is she responsible for the harm to the children?*

Freud identified early childhood as the location of sexual conflicts and desires and developed the idea of the Oedipus complex, where children have sexual wishes towards the parent of the other sex while being fearful of and hostile towards the same-sex parent. With a focus on boys, this model is named after Oedipus in Greek mythology, who unknowingly married his mother after a long separation. Freud argued that this complex was a fundamental relationship dynamic that could take different forms but was important in influencing adult personality and sexual expression. He also viewed children as being 'polymorphously perverse', that is, they are subject to many strong and varied sexual urges that are progressively regulated and repressed through social influences until a managed adult sexuality emerges. Children experience the sexual instinct through bodily touch, not just genital contacts and stimulations, and this diversity of pleasures is gradually limited through what is deemed to be acceptable or otherwise. Even then, Freud felt that there were battles to be had as an adult in controlling often dangerous, perverse and socially unacceptable sexual desires, leading to compromises and frustrations. Genital heterosexual coitus was the ultimate aim of adult sexuality, although achieving this and sustaining it was fraught with problems and possible deviations.

Freud explained perversions as those sexual expressions that did not accord with the normal genital heterosexual coitus in two main ways. The sexual *object* is that body which is desired, so an adult desire for sexual activity with children is a perversion of the sexual object that should be that of an adult of different sex. These deviations of the object are due to developmental issues in childhood, perhaps through learned experiences. The second mechanism at work is that of anomalies of sexual *aim*, where areas of the body other than the penis inserted into the vagina are found to be stimulating, including use of the mouth and anus as well as other forms of sexual expression such as exhibitionism. Thus Freud had a strong sense of what was normal in sexual expression, yet he was not moralistically condemnatory when describing other sexual behaviours. Denman (2004, p 69) explains this as:

> … [Freud] emphasises strongly that all sexual outcomes are a compromise between the sexual instinct, seen in some

sense as innocently diverse, and the demands of civilisation,
seen as the prohibiting parent writ large.

So as we have seen, although Freud may have a normative view of sexual expression, he viewed deviations from this in a rather benign way, the inevitable result of the titanic struggles between the inner and outer worlds, between terrifying unconscious forces and the brutal conforming demands of society. From a Freudian perspective, it is hardly surprising that sex has such a central place in our thinking, as it shadows our every move and thought, driving us on to achievement, but is also capable of being a destructive force.

The authors' experiences as lecturers of social workers and other social care professionals have led to the expectation that students have vague familiarity with the terminologies involved with Freudian ideas about the stages of human development. For example, people can generally state that someone is 'anal' when they mean that they are not expressing emotions, although there is little sense of understanding the context of this. Below are outlined the key stages of development created by Freud to demonstrate how important sex (in all its meanings) is to these categories.

Oral stage

A newly born infant is concerned primarily with feeding, leading to a focus on the mouth as the source of sensation and pleasure. This period lasts during the first year of life and the oral stage is the first layer of human development in the sense that all the stages have to be successfully and sequentially completed to progress to the next one. Failure to do so can have consequences in later life or make transitions more difficult. Followers of Freud have focused on some of the personality traits that can arise from different experiences of these transitions. Someone who was overstimulated or spent too long at the oral stage may well be overgenerous, gullible or optimistic, whereas someone who was deprived of oral stimulation may be more pessimistic and greedy.

Anal stage

As the infant develops, it is subjected to the pressures of toilet training and the awareness of control of excretion. The anus and defecation become sites and processes of pleasure, pleasure that is both physical and emotional, reinforced through parental/social praise and punishment for appropriate behaviours. Controlling the body through retention and expelling of faeces focuses the child on this area and how the child is toilet-trained can have a significant impact on future behaviour. Overemphasis with this stage can lead to the development of personalities that are rigid, ordered and obsessive, particularly about cleanliness. They can also have an unwillingness to let go, often represented by a reluctance to spend money and a preference for saving and hoarding. This stage occurs at the ages of about two to three.

Phallic/Oedipal stage

This stage lasts between the ages of about three to six and is a complicated development away from anal-focused sexuality towards genital sexual pleasure. The key element of this theoretical stage is the way in which children gain a particular awareness of their parents' physical differences and how they make sense of this. The Oedipus complex leads to desire for the other-sex parent; however, this changes during this period, as Freud maintained that boys become aware that mother does not have a penis and that they make sense of this by understanding that mother was a boy who challenged father, who then castrated her. This is a fundamental horror for the boy, who wishes to avoid castration at all costs, and he begins to identify with the father in order to reduce the potential for father to harm him. Sexual feelings (particularly as these have often been towards mother) are repressed and the child begins to develop controlling structures and mechanisms (the superego) to manage the tensions between their inner desires and the outer world. Girls are thought of differently in this theory; indeed, it is during the Oedipus complex that differences become constructed psychically. The girl realises that she has been castrated and that she has no hope of gaining the status of maleness. Envious of the penis and resigned to their lot, Freud suggests that women do not develop as strong a superego or moral sense as men do, as they have no need of such structures. Women accept that femininity and sexual passivity is their role and they can gain some compensation for their circumstances through possession of a penis by the proxy of their male child. In addition, women leave behind the immature pleasures of clitoral stimulation and accept adult vaginal orgasm.

In creating this model for women, Freud himself accepted that it was extremely difficult to imagine coming through this without some compromises and problems. Indeed, he developed his ideas about female sexuality further and posited that the ideal feminine state for a woman was a masochistic and narcissistic one, although he could accept that there were other variations on female sexuality, such as lesbianism and a complete rejection of sex.

Latency and genital stages

The terrors of the castration threat are internalised and sexual drives and expression are suppressed for the rest of pre-pubertal childhood, roughly from ages five to 12. Here, the sexual drives of children are hidden from themselves and others, controlled by an increasingly developed superego. The onset of puberty then leads to the genital stage, where interest in sexual expression and contacts triggers the development of adult sexuality.

Since Freud constructed the basis of his theory, there have been further developments, disagreements and derivations of these fundamentals, leading to other ways of approaching sex and sexuality, such as that of Jung and, particularly in the British context, Klein. Klein placed more emphasis on the mother and the breast as significant in the development of children and their sexuality, and she had a very strong view that a narrow form of heterosexual relationship was the normal and ideal bio-psychological state (Harding, 2001). This has led in the past to some psychotherapeutic courses refusing to accept lesbian and gay students on the grounds that they are flawed in their development, and a pronounced homophobic tendency within psychotherapy (Domenici and Lesser, 1995). Psychological explanations and understandings of sex and sexuality have force in our society and can be found in everyday social work practices and discussions. Some of the more involved theoretical approaches can now seem to be problematic, as we are increasingly comfortable (mainly due to feminist contestation) with questioning ideas that hold oppressive consequences for women. Thus although some of the concepts have permeated our ways of thinking, there are others that struggle to be heard in the face of changed social and academic knowledge and values.

Physical bodies

There is no doubt that physical differences between men and women exist, with obvious sexual organ differences but also a tendency for men to be larger and stronger. However, these are tendencies rather than absolutes and clearly there are some women who are larger and stronger than some men. In a functionalist way of thinking, these anatomical differences are designed to complement each other, with the sexual organs designed to perform specific (and obvious) functions. The penis is designed to enter the vagina to ensure reproduction, a clearly natural and evolutionary role that is self-evident. An evolutionary and biological approach would support the notion that as humans are animals this is the prime function of sexual activity, to propagate the species through reproduction, and that it is natural for women to seek penetration by the penis and men to seek to penetrate the vagina with it. Human sexual desire is, in this construct, linked to the obvious anatomical structures of the physical body.

However, the human body is not always as straightforward as it may at first appear and its structure does not always or absolutely support this functional understanding of sex. Take, for example, the clitoris, which is the pleasure-giving female sexual organ. In a functionalist perspective, this should be designed to encourage sexual pleasure in the context of sexual penetration for the purposes of reproduction, so it seems unusual that this organ should have been placed outside the body, rather than in a more obviously penetration-related position within the vagina. Is this a biological oversight or perhaps an indication that sexual pleasure is more than reproduction? The variety of bodily erotic experiences beyond simply genital contact is too large to outline here but indicates that sexual expression/experience within the body is very broadly based indeed, with the simple reproductive action being one of many. Penetrating a vagina with a penis is often viewed within a biological framework as being the only real sexual act as it is linked most clearly with reproduction, and this act can be privileged as the template for all sexual activity, the standard by which all other sexual acts are measured and the expectation of those who are performing sexually. This even extends to expectations of non-heterosexual activity, where penetration is viewed as so natural that it may be assumed that two men in a same-sex relationship will take penetrator–penetrated roles, despite their individual preferences. As Wilton (2004) has discussed, this leaves women who are in same-sex relationships with the expectation that they will try to construct the same sexual practice through artificial or other means. The natural image of penetration is so strong that it pervades assumptions and expectations of all sexual behaviour and influences the way in which those involved see themselves and are seen by others. Thus terms such as 'active' and 'passive' used to describe actors in sexual behaviour are not neutral words but are given a certain status, with those who are active viewed as masculine and powerful, whereas those who are passive are more feminine and less powerful. As we can see, these labels and attributes cross over into social expectations of gender, where the inferior social position of women may be supported by arguments about natural passivity, as evidenced by and through sexual practices.

After recently coming out as lesbian, Sharon had been genitally sexually assaulted by a female acquaintance after a night out. She had been threatened with extreme violence prior to the assault. Sharon was distraught and said that she felt as violated as when she had previously been raped by a man, when she had bravely gone to court to give evidence against him. Her attacker was charged with assault by penetration, as rape can only be committed by a man with his penis as defined in the 2003 Sexual Offences Act. Although the penalties for both offences are the same, Sharon was left feeling that her experience had been devalued by the legal definition.

What do you consider to be a hierarchy of sexual offences against the person? How may this affect your work with people who have been sexually assaulted? How may this affect your work with people who have been sexually abusive?

Biological difference

The physical body as the site of sexuality raises questions of normality that have consequences for people who may not fit these expectations. In the discussion above, there was a taking for granted that physical difference between men and women was fixed and obvious, yet this can be confounded by those people where this is unclear (hermaphrodites can have physical elements of both sexes) or where they feel that their body is of the wrong sex. In the former situation, a child born with genitalia that are not clearly male or female, caused by some unusual foetal developments, is now commonly called 'intersexed'. There are documented cases of forcing people into a specific gender role based on assumptions about their biological detail and the social need to ascribe a gender to a child that unfortunately have not always been helpful for the person (Colapinto, 2000). The idea of a 'core gender identity' has been developed, which posits that there is an intrinsic gender that is not always obvious but can be found and then medically corrected, a condition known as 'gender dysphoria'. However, too rigid an early gender ascription can create difficulties as the body is forced into a social role that may become biologically inappropriate as they age. Corrective surgery may be applied to modify ambiguous genitalia at too early a stage of development, which can create later physical problems. Trying to fit someone's body into a strict binary male–female divide does not always reflect the reality that human physiological diversity includes those who confound this either/or situation. A further difficulty has been that these ambiguous bodies have been the site of medical discussion and experiment about the influence of nature and nurture in human development, leading to a situation where '… the needs and wishes of the patients have come a poor second to academic debate' (Denman, 2004, p 229).

Transgendered people consider that their body is at odds with how they feel about their gender, which can lead to corrective surgical and chemical procedures to change the current body for one that more closely resembles that of the sex they feel most comfortable in (Bancroft, 1989). Such changes do not (currently) create a biologically complete body, as the sexual organs cannot be developed for reproduction, but the body can strongly resemble that of the preferred sex. Male genitalia can be removed and a vagina can be constructed; a penis can be created from other bodily tissues, although erections are problematic. The transgendered issue brings together questions of whether gender is biologically or socially constructed, or perhaps both. Is a male-to-female post-operative transsexual person now a woman, or is being a woman more than simply the physical body? Is it also the experience of being brought up a woman in society? Medical procedures have destabilised the certainty of the body as an indicator of a fixed notion of sex, which raises some important questions about how we make sense of sex and gender. These are questions that do have some significance for social work practice, as a discussion may need to be held to consider whether someone who was born male is appropriate for a women-only service, for example, a group for women experiencing domestic violence. It also raises questions of sexual identity; for example, is a man who has a sexual relationship with a male-to-female post-operative transsexual straight or gay?

Disabled bodies

The situation of disabled people regarding sex and sexuality has been given increasing attention, as there has been a growing concern at the way in which disabled people have been marginalised in society. Shildrick (2004) analyses how disabled people have been excluded from consideration of sexuality because of assumptions and expectations of being disabled. She argues that sex and sexuality have been silenced when talking about disabled people, that this is a topic that is beyond naming, as it does not fit with the dominant ways of thinking about how sex should be. This is partly due to issues of fertility and eugenics, where there is a history of preventing disabled people from procreating because of notions of racial purity, the expected burden on the state and the inability to care for children. It is also linked to impairment, where a singular notion of sex as heterosexual coitus may not be available (or indeed desirable) for some disabled people; thus there is an assumption that sex cannot happen or that, if it does, it is not proper sex. This idea of sex as one specific action reduces the rich complexity of sexual pleasures available to people, whether disabled or not, and is used as the normative measurement of all sexual activity.

The medical model of disability has contributed to 'othering' those people who have impairments through concentrating on problems and making comparisons with what is expected of the able-bodied norm. What people cannot do and how to assist the body in achieving normality has been a central focus of this approach, leading to the problem being located within the person and requiring treatment (wheelchairs, therapies, artificial limbs, drugs and so on) to rectify these deficiencies. Social work practice has been complicit in this through assessment and intervention strategies. However, the emergence of the social model of disability has questioned the ways in which the needs of disabled people are conceptualised and addressed, with an emphasis not on recreating a body in the image of an able-bodied norm, but on recognising that there are barriers to full participation located within the structures of society. These barriers can be attitudes, physical constructions and systems that lock disabled people into a victim position that requires help, and the approach looks for ways in which these barriers can be challenged, dismantled or changed to allow disabled people to participate more fully in society. This is not to ignore the often real physical difficulties that disabled people can experience with their bodies when functioning is impaired, but it does move the emphasis away from changing the person to recognising the importance of the environment (Shakespeare et al, 1996). Disabled people need to be recognised as sexual beings with all the complexities that this brings, including allowing for a rethinking of what constitutes sex to encompass a broader range of behaviours than a presumed norm.

As most people are only temporarily able-bodied (anyone can become physically impaired at any point in their lives), emotional problems can be created when this temporary status is changed. The negative sexual images of disabled people may generate anxiety when someone becomes impaired, leading to concerns about their future functioning as a sexual being. Providing support to counter these powerful inhibitors to leading a sexual life (if wanted) through accepting the sexuality of disabled people is an important consideration in working practices. The individual nature of impairments opens opportunities for new sexual behaviours that can be fulfilling, despite not fitting the narrow heteronormative expectation of sex.

Body problems

Although an essentialist and biological approach has limitations and consequences, there are times when the body may create difficulties. Most sexual performance problems seem to be emotional and psychological in nature, although the physiology of the body can be the cause of sexual difficulties and many people are unaware of the physical nature of these. Service users can be anxious about the sexual functioning of their bodies and should be encouraged to seek medical advice. However, it is helpful to know that some of these matters are well documented, as the ways in which we talk about sex do not always assist in calming fears.

> James has moderate learning difficulties and at 30 has begun a relationship with Jean, who also has learning difficulties. He is concerned about beginning a sexual relationship and says that he is drinking heavily to 'enhance my performance'. He has found that this does not work all the time and he has started to harm himself. Scared of doctors, he asks his social worker for advice on what to do.
>
> *How would you talk to James (and Jean) about this?*

For example, sexual desire in men can be reduced by the lowering of the androgen hormonal levels in the body, a process that occurs naturally with ageing. When people are generally unwell, their sexual desires can be affected. Anxiety can also play an amplifying part in sexual difficulties, as any occasional failure to perform can have emotional consequences that may inhibit future behaviour. If problems are painful and/or persistent, medical advice should be sought, as some physical conditions, including sexually transmitted diseases, can create difficulties. Pain for a woman during penetration can be caused by her not being sufficiently aroused or lubricated, or by physical damage to the pelvic ligaments or the ovaries by vigorous thrusting. Reduced oestrogen (a common result of the menopause) can affect the ability of the body to lubricate, causing pain.

Denman (2004) identifies other medical conditions that can have effects on sexual functioning, including diabetes, where the disease causes specific damage to blood supply that can compromise erections in men and lubrication in women (Bancroft, 1989). An awareness of this may be helpful to those working with people with diabetes, as this can be a major concern that is difficult to discuss. Heart diseases and high blood pressure can also place physical limitations on sexual exertion that can in turn increase anxiety and reduce sexual functioning. The interplay between the physical and the emotional is complex and can aggravate the situation. Mental illnesses and their pharmacological treatments can also have a deleterious effect on the libido and most of the current popular anti-depressants are known to have sexual problems as side effects for both men and women.

Further reading

Lancaster, R.N. and di Leonardo, M. (1997) *The Gender Sexuality Reader*, London: Routledge.

Wilton, T. (2000) *Sexualities in Health and Social Care: A Textbook*, Buckingham: Open University Press.

Summary

- Sexual behaviours are wide and varied, but subject to regulation by social, cultural and moral expectations.
- Talking about sexual behaviours can be difficult.
- One person's sexual preference may not be to another's taste.
- Children exhibit sexual behaviour and this creates adult anxiety.
- Essential understandings of sex and sexuality have powerful support and credence in our society.
- Biological explanations can be helpful in considering physical rather than emotional and psychological problems.
- Biological explanations may reflect more about the values of the definer than the reality of sex and sexuality.
- Binary male–female understandings of the body are a product of a way of thinking about the world, and accentuate differences that may be too exaggerated.
- Psychological explanations can have rigid templates of sexual development that impose a normative judgement on diverse sexualities.

TWO

Sex, sexuality and society

So far this book has outlined some of the biological ideas that inform our understanding of sex and sexuality. This chapter looks at how ideas have developed from the rather polarised debates about the influence of nature or nurture into ways that question the need to understand sex and sexuality through creating categories in which to place people. Some of the ways in which these ideas have been rethought are through the application of social constructionist and discourse theorising, recognising that how we talk and make sense of particular issues changes over time and that certain ways of talking and understanding are privileged over others. This has consequences for people's identities around sex, sexuality and gender, as we must ask questions about the truths we hold dear about the categories created by these ideas. Weeks (2003) has comprehensively outlined the range of theoretical understandings of sexuality, identifying that this is an area of competing knowledge that has changed and that at different times particular approaches have been favoured and/or marginalised. Power is central to this thinking – the power to define and allow what is known about a subject. Hicks (2005a, p 142) has outlined some of the key elements of this thinking with specific reference to sexuality and social work. As he states:

> The very term 'sexuality' is itself problematic because it is usually taken to refer to something possessed by a person, as in, 'what is your sexuality?'. This, of course, relies upon a way of thinking which divides bodies, desires, actions into a series of discrete 'types' such as 'the lesbian', 'the gay man', 'the bisexual', or 'the heterosexual'. However, while these terms appear simply to describe the way people are, 'lesbian', 'gay' and so on are actually socially achieved ideas that are part of a wider set of sexual discourses that regulate what can and cannot be known or said.

This challenges notions that there are types of (sexual) people that are easily recognised and, in social work, catered for, and it illuminates the range of differences within the categories lesbian, gay man, heterosexual and so on. Assumptions that, for example, all lesbians have basically the same needs, and therefore, once someone is identified as such, steps can be taken to meet them, are problematic in that a person's individuality is lost within the expectations of the label. Such categorisations tend to subsume the person within an identity that is often not of their own making, nor one they may wish to own. It also raises questions about what sort of things we describe as sexuality, for, as Plummer (1975) suggests, nothing is sexual until we name it so. A historical perspective on sex and sexuality is important here and the influence of Michel Foucault (see, particularly, 1990) is central to making sense of these matters. His notion of discourse is useful for social workers in considering how we come to talk about and make sense of sexuality. Hicks (2005a) has a helpful and clear explanation of the ways in which applying a Foucauldian discourse approach to sexuality and social work allows for the development of a more thoughtful and reflexive practice, and he quotes Cheek (2000, p 23) for a useful definition of discourse:

> Discourses create discursive frameworks which order reality in a certain way. They both enable and constrain the production of knowledge in that they allow for certain ways of thinking about reality whilst excluding others. In this way they determine who can speak, when, and with what authority, and conversely, who can not.

With this in mind, the rest of this chapter is approached in a critical way in exploring how social work knowledges about, and practices with, sexuality have particular implications for service users. This is not to say that these implications are necessarily good or bad (although some may well be more helpful and less discriminatory than others) but that whatever the approach there will be processes and consequences that require thoughtful reflection.

On a broader level, Carabine (2004, p 8) helpfully outlines some of the key elements of a social constructionist approach to understanding sex and sexuality as follows:

*   It rejects and challenges the essentialist view of sexuality as a natural, biologically determined force.
*   The focus is not on sexual acts but on the development of individual sexual identity, which is the result of a complex negotiation of social labelling and self-identification.

- The meanings people attach to sexual acts and behaviours are shaped by forces that are specific to that social context in which they are experienced, so how some things come to be called sexual or not is of interest.

This perspective allows us to reflect that the ways in which we think about the world may simply be the product of the ways in which our social context allows or encourages us to think, privileging some ideas over others. It can help social workers to consider how power may be operating to promote certain understandings and practices and disallow other modes of sense making. Social constructionist ideas challenge the fixed, inborn or innate explanations of sexual identities as being the product of dominant and powerful socially privileged modes of thinking. The previous chapter showed how dominant scientific explanations have laid claim to finding out the truth of sex and sexuality through investigation, yet this raised some difficulties from the aspect of scientific rigour but also about how these matters are conceptualised.

Carabine identifies that there are some differences within social constructionism about sex and the body, as there is a train of thought that accepts that there is such a thing as a sexual impulse that exists in itself but is moderated, channelled and expressed through social factors, whereas another strand views all sexual feelings and wishes as socially constructed and having no independent existence.

The social organisation of sex and sexuality

Weeks (2003) provided a useful structure for considering how sex and sexuality are influenced by social factors. This consists of five broad areas: kinship and family systems; economic and social organisation; social regulation; political interventions; and cultures of resistance.

Kinship and family systems

The family unit is often viewed as the basis of society and assumed to be fairly constant in how it operates. However, any cursory historical and comparative social investigation shows that family is subject to difference depending on where and when we look at it. Family takes different forms and can mean the Western nuclear family or may be expanded to take in a whole extended system of relatives. It can be reconstituted or sometimes not based on biological ties at all. Families are regulated by state policies about how they function, in marriage and divorce, age of consent and limitations on who is allowed to have sexual relationships. In the UK, there are differences in family organisation influenced by cultural factors of class and ethnicity, leading to social workers having to consider their importance when engaging with service users. Assuming that a family follows a specific pattern can lead to problems. For example, rules about the marriage of cousins may vary within families and cultures, and who constitutes a cousin may vary within cultures. There is not only difference, but there is also change, as what is acceptable (or not) has not remained static. Families are influenced and constructed through social forces.

Economic and social organisation

The ways in which economic patterns and changes have affected sex and sexuality can be illustrated by the changing economic position of women in our society. The work patterns of men and women have gone through significant upheavals, with a move from pre-industrial rural structures, to industrialisation and our current engagement with a globalised economy. Women have had opportunities to become economically active, leading to changes in their economic power and in expectations of their roles. Economics have influenced the types of jobs available for men and women, as well as changes in work patterns. These have in turn affected women's rights and fertility and the historical subordination of women has at least been challenged if not eradicated. This change has been mediated through class and ethnicity, but nonetheless has a significant impact on how sex and sexuality are constructed. Economic migration has also led to social diversity in attitudes to sex and sexuality and their regulation, as well as destabilising cultural patterns of sexual behaviour. The growth of sex trafficking, with economically poor people (mainly women) being brought to richer nations to be used by men, can also be viewed as a product of global economic and social change.

Social regulation

Sex and sexuality are regulated by social forces such as morality and beliefs that act as powerful determinants of what is allowed to be done, where, when and with whom. These informal ways of regulating will have been experienced by all readers of this book, as we learn at an early age what are appropriate gender expectations, what sexual activity is allowed and what pejorative names (and indeed actions) can be given to those who transgress these rules. These can be reinforced or influenced by more formal state interventions through legislation or policy. The case of abortion is helpful to consider here, as this is subject to strong personal, familial and cultural moral positions that affect the decision, as well as being regulated by specific legal frameworks.

Political interventions

The prevailing political context can affect sex and sexuality in very direct ways, through campaigns that make claims to the territory of sex. These include political movements to gain equality for women, lesbians and gay men, as well as socially conservative campaigns to regulate against what are seen as undesirable elements. The debate about the age of consent for gay men in the UK during the 1990s was the site of contested political agendas, some of which were more overtly party-political. Abortion has been used in a directly political way to differentiate political parties in the US, and there has been direct political action to regulate the behaviour of women in some countries (an extreme example being Afghanistan under the Taliban).

Cultures of resistance

Resistance to dominant social expectations of sex and sexuality has been recognised increasingly as having existed throughout history, as well as more recently. People have always found ways of subverting or transgressing restrictions, either individually or as part of movements, privately or publicly. Evidence exists that historically women have practised birth control despite the often severe legal consequences, and that lesbians and gay men have questioned their oppression in different ways over time. Feminism has a history of resistance to male domination through thought and deed, demanding that the subordination of women be acknowledged and challenged. In many cases, acts of individual and collective resistance have led to changes that have lessened the oppressive nature of the social organisation of sex and sexuality, challenging taken-for-granted assumptions that underpinned discriminatory attitudes, values and legislation.

Consider the five themes above. In what ways have each of these influenced your views on sex and sexuality?

Gender, race and class

Gender can be seen as the ways in which certain behaviours, attributes and expectations are ascribed to men and women and then performed in societies. It has been described by Oakley (1972, p 16) as '… a matter of culture: it refers to the social classification into "masculine" and "feminine"', and is usually contrasted with a fixed notion of biological sex. For example, the idea of the 'opposite sex' is widely held and often quoted in jest or sometimes with a sort of perplexed shrug, as people struggle (and fail) to understand the ways in which people who are not of their gender behave. Talking in this way reinforces difference between men and women almost to the point of being different species – the *Men are from Mars; Women are from Venus* arguments within the populist works of John Gray, for example. Yet biologically men and women are more similar than different, and the differences can be seen to be accentuated by social factors rather than being genetic or intrinsically natural. Bonvillain (1995) pointed out that if gender differences were natural, how men and women acted and what they were allowed to do would be similar across cultures and time, yet this is clearly not the case. Contemporary feminists such as Jackson and Scott (1996) have also questioned the essentialist, biologically determined views of gender and sexuality. Hood-Williams (1996) argued that historically men and women were viewed as variations on a single theme, rather than being thought of in terms of difference. Gendered attributes such as clothing, deportment, speech, mannerisms, hair and so on may be supported by arguments of naturalness, but there is clearly nothing within our DNA (yet identified) that specifies wearing a particular item of clothing. The rigidity of gendered dress codes can be experienced by anyone who dresses a baby in the 'wrong'-coloured clothing, where comment will be passed and assumptions made based on this colour coding. The clothing of particular societies varies and may well transgress gender when applied in different contexts. In Western societies men rarely wear something identified as a dress (the use of the kilt by Scottish men is an exception that is linked with displays of masculinity), yet similar garments are routinely worn by men in non-Western cultures without placing their notion of being a man in jeopardy. It is clear that there is no natural reason why Islamic women should wear a hijab, nor why men in Western societies would baulk at wearing a sarong in public (except perhaps on holiday). Judith Butler (1990) introduced the notion of 'gender performativity', identifying that ways of gendered being are socially and culturally constructed, reinforced by images and speech and enforced by social approbation and regulation. How we *do* our ascribed gender is influenced by and recreates socially acceptable categories and expectations. However, there is still a strong presumption that gender is natural and this is reinforced by aspects of social policy (to be revisited later).

> John and Sheila had been married for 20 years. He works full time and she works part time. Sharon and Darren have lived together for five years. She works part time and he is unemployed. Both couples wish to be considered as foster carers.
>
> *How confident do you think each couple is about their application? What issues may be concerning them? What do they think the social worker may be assessing? What assumptions have you made about them as you read this (sex/gender; class; ethnicity; disability; health; housing)?*

Although it can be argued that gender is the major arena in which sexual politics is played out, this is not to say that the male–female divide is absolute and all encompassing. There have been criticisms of the focus within gender for ignoring or marginalising differences within women and men as categories, particularly around class, race and (dis)ability. hooks (1996), for example, has been critical of the tendency for feminist explanations of power to be dominated by white, Western, bourgeois ways of thinking that marginalise the importance and experience of ethnicity and racism. Similarly, Skeggs (1997) has explored the importance of class in the lived experience of women and how a working-class identity can have limitations that individual women struggle against. Ethnicity and class can be complicating factors in understanding sex and sexuality, as there are powerful racist assumptions about black people that sexualise and make exotic what is different, as well as historical concerns about the unruliness of working-class sexuality. Thus black men can be viewed as more sexually dangerous and black women can be seen as more sexually voracious than a (presumed) white norm. This places black people in an ambivalent position of being endowed with often desirable physical qualities, yet categorised as being more naturalistic and primitive in their desires. The idea that non-white peoples are closer to nature is a strong one in Western thinking, supported by scientific understandings that generate a hierarchy of ethnicities and races and lead to beliefs in the animalistic sexuality of black peoples (Stoler, 1995). These beliefs can support the rape and sexual abuse of a black woman by casting her as sexualised, blaming her for provoking the assault or being oversexed, and can also racialise the aggressive sexual behaviour of an individual black man by reference to a supposed animal and uncontrollable nature. Edward Said (2003) has described the ways in which Europeans eroticised peoples of the Middle East and South Asia, ascribing qualities of sexuality that helped to construct otherness, in this case the notion of the 'Oriental'. This process has at its core a notion of Western culture as the norm and all other social expressions as perverse, primitive or underdeveloped. This racialisation of sexuality is reflected in some discussions about sexual assaults committed by black youths, where the reporting of their ethnicity has led to calls for a consideration of the sexism within black cultures. This linking of individuals committing offences to a perception of black culture as the root of the problem subsumes all black people into this category of dangerous and reduces cultures to (negative) monolithic stereotypes. A sexual assault by a white youth would not attract the same analysis of cultural deficit; these actions would be viewed as those of an individual and not a symptom of, or representative of, white culture. The highlighting of Asian men involved in a child sex abuse case in Bradford in 2004 led to the racialisation of what could be more accurately read as a problem of men abusing girls. Instead, the focus became one of Asian men abusing white girls, which was exploited by political racist groups and linked into simplistic images of a misogynistic culture and a threat to white people (Branigan, 2004). Such pejorative views deny the complexities and contestations within minority cultures and lock people into a fixed identity, making it harder to recognise and achieve change. Social workers were involved in this case through child protection and had to negotiate their way through such arguments and perceptions.

> Tariq was behaving in an inappropriate sexual manner with girls within the children's home. This was described by a (white) care worker as worrying but 'part of his culture ... he can't help himself due to the way he has been brought up to view girls'.
>
> *What expectations of gender, culture and 'race' are there here? What is the difference between ideas of cultural identity and of racial identity? How will this understanding of the behaviour help Tariq and others?*

Cultural relativism can also be used to justify poor sexual behaviour. For example, consider the following extract from an interview undertaken by one of the authors with a very articulate 16-year-old boy who had sexually abused younger boys:

> ... it's the fashion at the moment for paedophilia to be wrong. Even today, in some very distant cultures, like Papua New Guinea, there are practices where they still do that. And in Ancient Greece, they used to as well. And is it only a matter of time, if we span a cycle on of 2000 years, will paedophilia be rife and legal and accepted again ... It's easy to convince myself. I forget ... I know it's wrong at the moment.

In struggling to change his behaviour, he was able to claim cultural differences to support his abuse of others. Fortunately, he was able to work on this and to move from this unhelpful position, but it does indicate the ways in which images of difference can be utilised to support problematic behaviour.

Although gender is influenced socially, there are debates about whether it is helpful to take a position that that is all it is, a social construct, or whether it is important to remember that bodily differences exist between men and women and that these form the physical basis of the unequal treatment of women. If it is the former, then there is a danger that inequalities will be minimised, hidden or lost and women will once again be marginalised. The latter position may help us to keep a focus on the forces that divide men and women, doing so in differing ways and having differing consequences, that are prejudicial to women. Dunphy (2000, p 41) believes that it is useful to retain '... the analytical distinction between sex and gender while remaining fully aware that human anatomy and biology should never be treated as fixed and unproblematic...'. This allows us to be critical of the way in which binary approaches divide people, but understand that biology has a part to play in structures of inequality.

Categorising sexualities

We have already mentioned some ways in which people can be viewed in binary terms, that is, as a series of opposites with gradations in between, and this has been significant in how we have constructed notions of sexual types of people, in particular the homosexual–heterosexual (or lesbian/gay–straight) divide. Other binary divides include man–woman, black–white and able-bodied–disabled, all of which represent a mode of thinking that is trying to make sense of people through creating categories of opposites. This is so powerful that we often take it for granted that these categories exist; that they are to be found naturally. Such binary ideas are not equally weighted; they tend to privilege one end of the spectrum as the norm against which others are measured and tend to fix identities. Change is not easily accommodated within these axes and people are forced into being 'either/or', with perhaps occasional places in between. This approach assumes that such categories are stable and unitary, yet we know that these labels are not as definite as they are claimed to be. Each of the binary poles assumes sameness, that someone can be identified as black or white, gay or straight. But blackness and whiteness cover a huge range of differences within themselves, and how do we define someone as straight if they have occasional emotional feelings towards someone of their own sex? If a woman leaves an other-sex marriage to enter into a relationship with another woman, has she always been lesbian or should she be categorised as bisexual to reflect the range of relationships over time? Contemporary critical perspectives have questioned whether this way of organising knowledge about people is helpful, as it leads to particular practices that reinforce dominant power relations, and 'queer theory' in particular has emerged to critique the binary divide between homosexuality and heterosexuality (Seidman, 1994). The term 'queer' has had negative connotations, but has been (re)claimed within queer theory to describe:

> ... a newly emerging set of commentaries, rather than a coherent school of thought [that] ... seeks to contest the binary opposition between heterosexuality and homosexuality, and 'heteronormativity', that is, the power relations that constitute heterosexuality as normative. (O'Brien, 1999, p 143)

The normative assumption within general explanations of sex and sexuality is that something called heterosexuality is common, natural and desirable; a state of being that makes sense through biology and is the taken-for-granted norm. However, heterosexuality has been subject to much scrutiny, particularly from feminist, radical and postmodern perspectives, which has led to a rethinking of what this actually means (Richardson, 1996). On one level, it refers to other-sex desire, the sexual attraction between a man and a woman. Yet heterosexuality is larger than this, it is the ways in which sexuality and gender (and indeed ethnicity and ability) play out in our society. It can regulate what sexual behaviours are favoured or not; it can tell you how old your partner should be; it can enforce where you have physical sex (as well as telling you what constitutes sex); it can privilege marriage and devalue other arrangements; and it can place fertility as the pinnacle of sexual achievement (Kitzinger and Wilkinson, 1993). Thus our heterosexuality is 'differentiated': within other-sex desire, it regulates what value is given to different sorts of relationships. A good example is the decision that some people have to make whether to get married or not. There are still advantages (financial, legal and social) to getting married, based on assumptions of the proper way to conduct relationships. A social constructionist approach would see heterosexuality as a series of discourses that place a boundary around what is known (and allowed to be known) about sex and sexuality, and it has a history and it varies from place to place. This particular narrow understanding of heterosexuality is a powerful one in Western (and indeed other) societies and is supported (and recreated) by and through laws, policies and practices, not least by social work practices. It is 'institutionalised' (O'Donnell, 1999) through 'heteronormativity', that is, the ways in which this heterosexuality is made the norm against which all other sexual relationships are judged. There is increasing discussion that perhaps we would be more helpful to people by thinking in terms of 'heterosexualities', rather than one notion of heterosexuality, as this frees us from the restraints imposed by a limited model and more accurately reflects the lived experiences of service users, as well as allowing us to value differences.

> *Make a list of all the characteristics associated with heterosexuality. How does it work? Where does it happen? What forms does it take?*

Our understanding of heterosexuality is influenced by attempts to make sense of sexual behaviour in the 19th century, based in the scientific models dominant at that time. The term homosexual had been invented in the middle of that century to describe and categorise someone who had a sexual preference for their own sex. By the end of the century, there had developed a need to describe the binary opposite of this, and the heterosexual was created (Katz, 1990). The work of Foucault (1990) is influential in understanding this process, as he explained the construction of the homosexual through the need to categorise and control. The heterosexual and heterosexuality were in many ways named and described in opposition to the homosexual and homosexuality, creating two distinct and separate types of people, whereas previously there had only been sexual behaviours and moral choices. This is the move, supported by scientific and social ideas of the time, to place people within a taxonomy of typologies, a listing of ways that people were allowed to be through categorisation by expert knowledge. The consequence has been that a notion of how a normal heterosexual behaves has arisen, which is in opposition to qualities supposedly associated with the homosexual. Social ideas of the qualities a real man is expected to display can be linked to this rejection of homosexual behaviours, although these are often based on a specific, stereotypical and narrow reading of the homosexual.

Simon's foster carers were keen to support him when he 'came out' as gay to them. They wanted him to make career choices where there would be less prejudice, so he was encouraged to take a course in nursing as 'there are lots of gays doing that and he is less likely to be discriminated against'.

As Simon's social worker, how would you respond to this? What assumptions are being made about gay men (and nursing)? How would you build on the concern of the foster carers to do their best for Simon?

This heterosexuality has been critiqued in several ways, with some writers (especially feminist and pro-feminist) being particularly focused on deconstructing how power operates within heterosexuality as an institution, seeking to illuminate this and distancing the structure from the sexual desires of individuals (see, for example, Hearn and Ford, 1991; Kitzinger and Wilkinson, 1993; Jeffreys, 1996). This challenging of the naturalness of power imbalances within heterosexuality (power imbalances that favour men) has opened up spaces to reconstruct other-sex relationships in a more egalitarian frame. However, there has also been a view that heterosexuality is so firmly and rigidly structured in gender that no amount of tinkering would enable women to achieve equality within this, leading to some women withdrawing from heterosexuality completely and embracing radical lesbianism (Wittig, 1992).

Heterosexuality is so taken for granted in our society that we often overlook it, forgetting that it exists and allowing it to be invisible. This leads to other sexualities being made hyper-visible because of their perceived difference from the norm. Social work practice is not immune to this refusal to see heterosexuality and can forget that there is a range of sexual ways of being that need to be considered and valued. Heterosexuality can enforce its will and make itself the norm through quite crude mechanisms. A man and a woman walking down the street holding hands may not attract so much as a glance, yet the response to two men would be somewhat different, except possibly in certain geographic safer spaces. There is evidence that lesbian and gay people can take great care to hide their sexuality in public spaces, not because they have not come to terms with their sexuality, but because of a justifiable fear of physical and emotional violence. Indeed, service users may allow social workers to assume that they are heterosexual to avoid the probable complications of negotiating how the worker may judge their non-heterosexuality (Brown, 1998). For example, lesbian and gay service users may well be wary of professionals given their general experience of an often hostile world, particularly those people in positions of structural power who hold theoretical, institutional or moral views that marginalise them. The dominance of psychodynamic theoretical perspectives in past social work training may well lead some workers to consider lesbian and gay sexualities as problematic, the product of developmental difficulties and requiring some therapeutic input in order to change (Kline, 1972). Brown (1998) has outlined how some of the theories used by social workers pathologise lesbians through constructing ideas of deficit and deviance, leading to judgements that are usually negative and supported by particular theoretical evidence. The developmental approach of Erikson (1948) is still popular in social work, yet has a pronounced heteronormative bias that ignores the institutional prejudice that lesbian and gay people experience (Crain, 1985). Homosexuality was only declassified as a psychiatric disorder by the American Psychiatric Association in 1973, and even then the vote to do so was strongly contested by a significant minority who believed that it should remain abnormal. Social workers who hold strong moral or religious beliefs that may well have led them into working with people in the first place may struggle to give a good service to people who are discriminated against by these beliefs, be they lesbian, gay or indeed expressing any sexuality that does not conform to a concept of normality.

Two social workers working in adoption refuse to assess any lesbians or gay men as prospective adopters due to their belief that this would be inappropriate for the child. They provide evidence for their belief by a particular interpretation of their religion.

What do you think should be the appropriate response to their actions?

1. *Support their right to their beliefs.*
2. *Provide additional training to allow them to understand the evidence about lesbian and gay adoptions.*
3. *Transfer them out of children's services to work with another service user group.*
4. *Discipline them on the grounds of professional misconduct.*

For a debate about the above, see Pearce and Smith (2003).

Social work has engaged with sexuality in ways that reflect dominant thinking about categories and types. We have already seen how heterosexuality (or a particular view of it) is accepted as normal and taken for granted, yet the whole concept of categorisation and labels can be questioned as being a product of a way of thinking. This can be seen in the ways in which dealing with sexuality has been approached in social work education. As in wider society, social work education (where it has been at all interested) has tended to focus on sex and sexuality as an area of problems to be understood and solved. Social work is a 'magpie profession', influenced by the knowledge base of other disciplines, and in its early incarnation was very focused on an individual pathological and medical approach that accepted the dominant explanations for sexual behaviours. Heterosexuality has received little attention for the reasons previously discussed, but non-heterosexuality has been the focus of much concern and writing, with gay and lesbian sexualities being the ground over which much of the debate has been played.

Language is important, however, and it is worth rehearsing some of the ways in which language has been marshalled to talk about what we currently call lesbian and gay (not forgetting bisexual and transgendered) people. This chapter has identified how the words heterosexual and homosexual were constructed to describe *types* of people, as if science had finally discovered that these categories existed. However, the 19th-century debates around the creation of the label homosexual reflected some of the debates about the essential nature of sexuality, with some leading sexologists (scientists focusing on investigating sex and sexuality) of the time using this label to argue for the naturalness of same-sex desire, and therefore for the acceptance of homosexuals as a part of the human sexual condition. In arguing such a position, they hoped for acceptance, but found that their arguments were used to medicalise and marginalise people, accentuating difference from the privileged norm of heterosexuality. Thus the term homosexuality became a vehicle for oppression rather than liberation, which accounts for the hostility of many contemporary lesbian and gay people to this label. It is a term imposed on people, with an associated pathology that leads to prejudicial practices, including spurious cures and expected ways of behaving, and always compared unfavourably with the mainstream heterosexuality. Uncritical use of the term can be seen as failing to recognise the (negative) discourses attached to it, thereby supporting continued structural oppression of lesbian and gay people. We suggest that social workers in their commitment to social justice should treat such terminology with caution, and look to the language favoured by service users, who are after all the experts in their lives.

In engaging with sex and sexuality, new words and concepts have appeared that are frequently used in the social work context. 'Homophobia' is a term that has developed to describe discriminatory views and actions against lesbian and gay people, and people who hold such views are 'homophobes' (Weinberg, 1972). This can be a useful term to identify what are clearly oppressive practices, yet it can create difficulties when applied uncritically, as it creates a type of person, the homophobe, who is given certain characteristics that do not recognise complexity. People may well hold views that are prejudicial, but these are influenced by environment and may not be consistent. There may be an acceptance of gay marriage (the arguments about which will be revisited later) but a rejection of fostering by gay men. Indeed, some individual lesbian and gay people may hold views that appear to be at odds with a social justice agenda of equality, perhaps having expectations of gender that are essentialist and do not comfortably accept roles outside these stereotypes. This can be seen as internalised oppression, where people absorb the negative views about them held by the wider society, but this notion implicitly assumes that there is a right way to act and believe as a lesbian or gay man, which can lead to a rather patronising dismissal of their views. Locking someone into an identity as a homophobe locates the problem as one of personal pathology, rather than the product of complicated social factors, and reduces the space for change. The terms can reduce anti-gay and lesbian prejudice to an individual and personality problem, rather than a social, structural matter, thus once again avoiding questioning the broader picture of how sex and sexuality are constructed within society. This is not to deny the existence of political movements that can be accurately described as being homophobic, and Hicks (2003) has charted the ways in which conservative Christian organisations have sought to attack the acceptability of lesbian and gay parenting through often crude caricatures, stereotypes and selective use of research evidence. 'Heterosexism' is another relatively new term that has been used to describe the ways in which heterosexuality is privileged and promoted as the norm through social (and personal) processes. Again it may serve a useful purpose in naming certain views and behaviours as excluding, marginalising or ignoring non-heterosexualities, but can also be problematic when used to label a person, rather than their actions or structural discrimination.

Hicks (2005a) has outlined how social work has attempted to challenge the oppression of lesbian and gay people through questioning pathologising discourses such as the linking of same-sex desire as a psychiatric disorder, but that there have been consequences in the way that newer models have conceptualised sexuality. These newer models have developed an understanding of lesbian and gay sexuality as an issue of the rights of a minority; similar to the ways in which ethnicity has been thought of in terms of majority–minority groups. Arguments for equality have been made on the basis of 'different but equal': that the rights of minority groups should be protected from the oppression of the majority. This approach has been well intentioned, a drive to confront the gross prejudice that existed (and still exists) against people who have same-sex relationships. However, this is predicated on the notion that there is a separate, distinct and easily identifiable group called lesbian or gay, which has characteristics that allow for a clear identity. It is a model based on essentialist principles similar to those that created the category homosexual and still emphasised difference. Mallon (1999, p 23) developed this theme of what Hicks (2005a, p 149) has termed an ethnic identity approach by suggesting that, in order to work effectively with lesbian and gay people, social workers needed to engage with '... knowledge of the history, culture, traditions and customs, value orientation, religious and spiritual orientations, art and music, of lesbian and gay communities'. This assumes that there is a separate cultural identity based on a fixed sexual difference, yet there are difficulties with this. It tends to view lesbian and gay people as undifferentiated, immune to structures such as race, gender, ability and so on. It ignores the ways in which different societies at different times and places make sense of sexuality, subsuming these into a notion of a discrete population with its own needs. It leaves unsaid the assumption that Western notions of an identifiable gay community are the proper outcome of liberated lesbian and gay people, and that failure to be part of this culture is a matter of external and internal oppression. Lesbian and gay people are taken out of the mainstream and placed within yet another space that may not be of their individual choosing. This is not to say that people cannot find support and solace within spaces that help them to feel proud of who they are and indeed it may be useful to take a stance in the face of oppression, but this approach allows society conveniently to sidestep questions about the divisive nature of such binary thinking, reinforcing a heterosexual–homosexual divide that allows mainstream heterosexuality off the hook of criticism.

> Your local authority wishes to act in the best interests of all citizens by including the following question in an assessment for the needs of older people: 'Are you lesbian/gay?'
>
> *What are the assumptions behind including this question? What may be some of the consequences of asking this question? What differences in service delivery may result from answering 'yes' to the question?*

Within social work the ethnic identity approach has been most clearly influential in anti-discriminatory practice (ADP), as articulated, for example, by Thompson (1993). ADP has been the preferred model of values-in-practice on many social work courses, promoting a way of understanding structural oppression and how to combat this. The model depends on agreed notions of identifiable difference, with groups of structurally oppressed people homogenised (black, women, disabled and so on) as having shared meaning to their lives. Interestingly, as Hicks (2005a, p 149) has pointed out, lesbian and gay concerns were marginalised in this construct, as there was a tendency to create a hierarchy of types of oppression with issues of sexuality at the bottom of the list of priorities. There was also the problem that as these groups were identified, they prioritised one aspect of identity (for example, being disabled) and struggled to make sense of the differences within these groups (being disabled and black, and a woman, and lesbian and so on). The very real differences between the experiences of gay men and lesbian women through gender were also subsumed into a 'lesbianandgay' agenda that tended to gloss over the different impact of social structures. Weeks (1985, p 203) described this as:

> Lesbians and gay men are not two genders within one sexual category. They have different histories, which are differentiated because of the complex organisation of male and female identities, precisely along lines of gender.

A consequence of seeing people as a label was explored by Brown (1998), who identified that many social workers approached lesbian and gay service users as lesbian and gay first and as individuals with their own needs, strengths and uniqueness second, leading to practices that accentuated difference and made their sexuality the central marker for all subsequent interventions. This may have been due to genuine concerns to ensure that issues of oppression were not marginalised, yet had the outcome of making this label the prime focus of concern to the exclusion of others. Hicks and McDermott (1999) found evidence that lesbian women assessed as foster or adoptive carers had their sexuality centralised by social workers, rather than a focus on their childcare skills and other relevant matters that a (presumed) heterosexual applicant would be subjected to. Conversely, some social workers ignored issues of sexuality with lesbian applicants completely, perhaps in a belief that to raise this would be discriminatory or through lack of confidence in talking about it, thus failing to allow for discussion of what could be important social aspects of their lived experience. If someone is experiencing direct discrimination due to homophobia, it may be important to know what strengths they have developed to deal with this and how these can be transferred into providing good childcare.

Constructive practice

Practices based on modernist assumptions about sex and sexuality make sense of complex behaviours by breaking them down into manageable categories, which in turn influence the ways in which risk assessments are undertaken and 'appropriate' interventions selected. This has the benefit of ensuring that professionals have a common language for talking about sex and sexuality. Unfortunately, this often differs from how individual service users experience their lives; they are not simply sexual beings and do not fit easily into the limited categories available, nor necessarily benefit from approved interventions. Postmodern analyses deconstruct these categories but the sheer complexity revealed by these analyses can seem overwhelming to practitioners. For example, how does a worker attend to all the anti-discriminatory practice issues in the instance of a black heterosexual woman beating up her white male partner or a white homosexual male carer emotionally abusing his HIV positive partner? These examples confound dominant expectations of gender and sexuality and leave workers with difficulties in making sense of and responding to such behaviour. Simply *de*constructing theoretical perspectives can overwhelm practitioners because critiquing established practice seems to offer little in the way of alternative *re*constructions. However, a constructive practice based on postmodern thinking is emerging and this chapter outlines some of the ways in which this works in order to provide practitioners with the skills and knowledge to engage with the complexities of recognising difference while being respectful and effective and responding to individual circumstances.

Within current social work practice there have been two main approaches that can be said to be influenced by postmodern thinking: narrative therapy and solution-focused therapy. The former has been developed by Michael White and David Epston (1990) and the latter by practitioners at the Brief Therapy Family Center in Milwaukee (De Shazer et al, 1986). Narrative therapy is concerned with deconstructing the problems that have been ascribed to people through the process of clinical categorisation, taking care to consider the oppressions that people have been subject to by their status in society such as race, class and gender. Solution-focused approaches do not consider either of these issues as central (although they may well emerge during therapeutic discussion); instead, they are based on research into what works in therapy, claiming that service users found it most helpful when a future- and strengths-oriented perspective was adopted. Both therapies resist explanations and categorisations in a search for understanding service users as unique individuals with unique experiences and unique strengths and solutions to their current difficulties. In both therapies, language is central. In solution-focused practice, the emphasis is on listening to service users' specific accounts of their lives, including the words they use. At no point is there any interpretation of what is being said. For example, although the service user may seem to fit a certain pre-defined category, the therapist puts this on one side to elicit a full account that will allow that person's unique experience of that category to emerge. Thus therapy will be tailored to that person's unique strengths rather than their categorisation, as there will always be exceptions to the dominant explanation.

A narrative therapeutic approach goes further in that it actually engages with and challenges dominant explanations and discourses, as these are seen as ways in which professionals can unwittingly reinforce unhelpful stereotypes, and ignore structural oppressions and unique experience that may well include a story of heroic resistance to circumstances (Jenkins, 1990). Both therapies regard resistance as a useful resource rather than a hindrance to professional endeavour.

This way of thinking has influenced how the authors practise and how the following chapters will be presented, using examples based on the authors' professional experience. Thus the reader will find no simple answers; instead, the complexities of sexual behaviours are explored. This is achieved through presenting some examples that are broad in their scope (for example, the effects of ageing), and at other times focusing on very specific examples (such as the assessment of prospective lesbian and gay adopters). It is suggested that moving away from dealing with people as categories and towards engaging with people as complex individuals is the key to good social work practice.

Further reading

Nye, R.A. (1999) *Sexuality: A Reader*, Oxford: Oxford University Press.

Weeks, J. (2003) *Sexuality* (2nd edn), London: Routledge.

Summary

- Social constructionist approaches allow for the consideration that sex and sexuality are heavily influenced by social factors.
- Sex and sexuality have different meanings at different times and in different places.
- Binary thinking can reduce complexities and produce categories that have a hierarchy.
- Heterosexuality has been increasingly problematised as privileged, narrow and taken for granted.
- The ways in which we conceptualise and talk about sex and sexuality have consequences for policy and practice.
- Deconstructing established practice can be unhelpful to the hard-pressed practitioner when there is no attempt made to offer alternative reconstructions.
- The most useful reconstructions for practitioners are those that use service users' language, experience, knowledge and strengths.
- Solution-focused and narrative therapies offer a constructive way of understanding and responding to the complexities of human sexuality.

THREE

Sex, sexuality and social policies

Social workers operate within a context of state policies that heavily influence what is allowed to be done, with whom, where and when. Welfare policies are structured in ways that can appear to be benign and neutral, yet they have implicit and explicit assumptions about sex and sexuality that permeate the ways in which social work practice is undertaken. Carabine (2004, p 2) points out that '... social policy does not have to be specifically concerned with sexuality for it to "speak" of sexuality and for it to regulate sexual relations and behaviour'. Chapter Two has identified how heterosexuality is institutionalised and this chapter now turns to some of the ways in which our social policies suggest, insinuate and demand that there are only certain types of sex and sexuality that should be favoured.

The prime location of this institutionalisation is within the family, or a specific notion of what a family should be. Legal, cultural and social privilege is given to supporting (heterosexual) marriage and the production and nurturing of children, with the nuclear family viewed as the basic element of society. In the UK, but also in many other countries, this support for a particular social institution has a history that has left a legacy that we still engage with today. Doolittle (2004) outlines the historical development of this in a clear way, bringing feminist perspectives to illuminate the ways in which gender has been conceptualised in policies. The very construction of the welfare state was premised on the husband as financial provider and the wife as an adjunct to him, with tax and benefit incentives to marry and to produce (legitimate) children, as well as assuming that women would be dependent on their husbands' welfare contributions. This history of state support can be seen to be positive in ensuring that people did not suffer the hardships of extreme poverty that had blighted sections of the population, yet the rationale for structuring around marriage included the need to prevent people from becoming a burden on the state. The debates and arguments about lone mothers that we have seen played out particularly during the 1990s have their resonances in history, with concerns expressed in the 19th century at the cost to local communities of unwed (working-class) mothers and their illegitimate children. Women were seen as needing to be supported by the fathers of their children through the framework of marriage, which until relatively recently was a legally binding contract that could only be broken in extreme circumstances. Assumptions were made about gender roles and in particular the role of women as being domestic, with the home viewed as a private sphere that only warranted state intervention when matters became too problematic. Feminist scholarship has argued that this gendered expectation has placed women in caring roles that have reduced the need for state expenditure, expecting Herculean tasks to be undertaken in the difficult circumstances of the nuclear family. These important functions have been under- and devalued, making women's contributions invisible and privileging the public space inhabited by men.

The development of welfare policies has been influenced by ideas about sexuality in its broadest sense, in that heterosexuality (a man and a woman in a long-term monogamous marriage; man as economically active; woman providing domestic and emotional support, raising children, caring for older relations) was presumed to exist and to be the natural state of being that was used as the yardstick against which welfare provision was measured (Weeks, 1989). Welfare benefit provision has always been assessed through this mechanism and, although there have been some changes, this is still the case in current systems. An example of this is the way in which the notion of a heterosexual married couple is used to describe other relationships, so there are references within government guidance accepting that people can live together in a variety of circumstances without getting married, but making sense of this through comparison with marriage and thus privileging the state of marriage. The Carer's Allowance Claim Form (DWP, 2006, p 4) explains it as:

> We use partner to mean
> - A person you are married to or a person you live with as if you are married to them or
> - A civil partner or a person you live with as if you are civil partners

The relationship status affects the assessment of benefit, with assumptions being made about married couples (in particular about caring) that have also influenced how the new civil partnership legislation functions. Social work assessment procedures can also make assumptions about the way in which relationships are presumed to work and it is useful to reflect on how social policies influence how social workers respond to service users.

Stanley is 86 and Iris is 79. They have been together for 57 years and have three children, seven grandchildren and four great-grandchildren. Stanley has increasing difficulty with mobility. As a social worker, you have been invited to undertake an assessment of their needs.

List the assumptions you have made when reading this scenario, including in your assessment strategy. How are they influenced by presumptions of heteronormativity?

Social policies can assist in normalising certain ways of being through more direct regulation. The law has been used to enforce sexual boundaries through proscribing what is acceptable, when, where and how. This has been the case with constructing sexual offences (which we will focus on later) but also in other spheres. For example, legislation has restricted access to fertility treatment by single and/or lesbian women through emphasising the need for fathers (DH, 1990) and the 1988 Local Government Act (Section 28(1)) stated that local authorities should not 'intentionally promote homosexuality or publish material with the intention of promoting homosexuality'. Although since repealed, this latter legislation impacted on social work practices mainly through creating confusion and anxiety about what could and could not be discussed with children and young people or whether accepting lesbian and gay foster carers constituted 'promoting'.

Changes in legislation have reflected some of the changes in social attitudes about sex and sexuality, but these have not always been consistent and have created new regulatory frameworks. The 2004 Civil Partnership Act introduced a specific legal relationship for same-sex couples that gave similar benefits (social, legal, financial) as married other-sex couples. This has been hailed as a significant acceptance of same-sex relationships that counters some of the gross injustices experienced by lesbian and gay people. Same-sex couples can now have their relationship formally recognised and accrue rights and responsibilities similar to those of married other-sex couples. Interestingly, this aims for equality with heterosexual marriage, using the construct of marriage as a template and ideal, which has raised questions about the way in which same-sex relationships are now regulated. Smith (1994) discussed how lesbian and gay people were differentiated into good and bad through social policies and practices, the *good* being people who kept their sexuality private, had a monogamous relationship and did not behave in a manner likely to challenge accepted gender and sexuality roles, and the *bad* those who did not behave in this prescribed way, perhaps by choosing to have multiple sexual partners and behaving in ways that confronted expectations of gender. Civil partnerships can be seen to be encouraging conformity to the ideal of the good lesbian or gay man, based on heteronormative discourses of long-term monogamy, financial security and independence, and, indeed, the proper raising of children. The guidance for civil partnerships explicitly highlights the financial aspects of the contract as partners have 'a duty to provide reasonable maintenance for you and your partner and any children of the family' (Women and Equality Unit, 2005, p 6). Civil partnerships provide a formalisation of relationship that is not available to other-sex couples who choose not to marry, which raises questions of equity and inevitable comparisons. Are we seeing the creation of a hierarchy of recognised relationships, with those who choose to make legal commitments (marriage/civil partnership) viewed as more stable, loving and *good*?

The privileging of marriage within social policy extends in very practical ways to parenting and the raising of children through financial and legal mechanisms. Parental responsibility (that is, who is defined in law as being responsible for the welfare and upbringing of a child) is subject to this regulation. Consider the following extract from government advice.

Box 3.1: How unmarried fathers can get legal responsibility

Unmarried fathers can acquire parental responsibility for their children in several different ways, depending on when their children were born.

For children born before 1 December 2003, unmarried fathers can get parental responsibility by:

- marrying the mother of their child or by obtaining a parental responsibility order from the court;
- registering a parental responsibility agreement with the court or by an application to court.

For children born after 1 December 2003, the situation is different. Unmarried fathers can get parental responsibility by:

- registering the child's birth jointly with the mother at the time of birth – this is now quite common and many parents choose to do this;
- re-registering the birth if they are the natural father;

- marrying the mother of their child or by obtaining a parental responsibility order from the court;
- registering with the court for parental responsibility.

Source: Direct.gov.uk/Parents (2006)

The changes in the legal position of fathers have recognised that marriage is less a definer of parental interest in children than was previously assumed. Marriage was seen as the natural way of acknowledging paternity, and is still the only way to gain parental responsibility without specific actions focused on the child through registration. Marrying the mother automatically gives legal rights over the child, whereas a choice not to marry requires additional (bureaucratic) actions to demonstrate a commitment to parental responsibility. Thus we can still view the legal framework as making assumptions about the state of marriage regarding the welfare of children.

Further reading

Carabine, J. (ed) (2004) *Sexualities: Personal Lives and Social Policy*, Milton Keynes/Bristol: Open University Press/The Policy Press.

Summary

- Social welfare policies are often based on assumptions about sex and sexuality, usually constructed around heteronormativity.
- Social policies support, regulate and exclude aspects of sex and sexuality.
- Social work operates in the context of social policies that influence how services and practices are delivered.

Part Two
Sexual well-being

This section examines the implications of government guidance on sexual well-being for social workers. The benefits of sexual health across the lifespan are outlined and populations vulnerable to poor sexual health are identified. There then follows a discussion of how social workers can develop their skills and knowledge of legal frameworks to promote better sexual health in different service user groups and settings. Both personal and public sexual health issues are covered, and further information sources are listed. Chapter Four examines government guidelines on sexual well-being and the implications of this for social work practice. Chapter Five focuses on the role of the social worker in developing sexual well-being and promoting safety in children and young people. Chapter Six examines the role of the social worker in promoting sexual well-being in adults in vulnerable situations.

FOUR

Sexual health

Government guidance increasingly links emotional and sexual well-being, thereby expanding the social work role. Two major concerns put the sexual health of the nation on the government agenda: the increased rates of sexually transmitted diseases, particularly HIV, and the rising rate of unintended pregnancies, particularly in young, unmarried women. But sexual health is not just concerned with the prevention of disease and pregnancy, as the Department of Health recognises:

> Sexual health is an important part of physical and mental health. It is a key part of our identity as human beings together with the fundamental rights to privacy, a family life and living free from discrimination. Essential elements of good sexual health are equitable relationships and sexual fulfilment with access to information and services to avoid the risk of unintended pregnancy, illness or disease. (DH, 2001a, para 1.2)

Nusbaum and Rosenfeld (2004) identify the benefits of good sexual health as:

- a link with the future through procreation;
- a means of pleasure and procreation;
- a sense of connection with others;
- a form of gentle, subtle or intense communication;
- enhanced feelings of self-worth;
- a contribution to self-identity.

Frequent and enjoyable sexual intercourse is a significant predictor for longevity (Palmore, 1982) but, paradoxically, people need to be physically and emotionally healthy to enjoy this important component of well-being. Sexual activity is denied many people on the grounds of their inability to sustain relationships or the unavailability of opportunity to make intimate relationships. Even for those in loving relationships, it can be disturbed by psychosocial issues, injury, illness, loss, medication or drug use. It follows then that protecting, supporting and restoring sexual health is an important component of social work, yet many social workers consider it to be a health rather than a social work issue. Their training reflects this, with modules on the broader social aspects of sexuality, such as the inequalities experienced by gay and lesbian people and the trauma resulting from sexual abuse, but little on the everyday risks involved in making sexual choices and the effects of loss, grief, illness, age and disability on sexual functioning.

Why sexual health is part of the business of social care

Quite simply, sexual health is a key area of social work because there is a clear relationship between sexual ill health, poverty and social exclusion. Thus the people who make up the service user population of social work are most at risk of unintended pregnancy, sexually transmitted disease and unfulfilling sexual lives. The Department of Health suggests that many people lack the information they want and need to make informed choices that will affect their sexual health but it would be naive of social workers to presume that increased access to information through sex education in schools and the provision of one-stop clinics will increase choice and reduce risky behaviour.

The complexities of 'choice' in sexual behaviour are illustrated by the authors' experience of working with a group of 14- to 15-year-old women at risk of being recruited into sex work through the introduction of drugs (Milner, 2003, 2004b). These young women were disadvantaged in a number of ways: they had experienced either physical or sexual abuse in early childhood; they were living in families which were emotionally unsatisfying, and from which they periodically ran away; they had been excluded from school; they had been either treated for depression or were actively self-harming; and they were associating with older men who were introducing them to drug and alcohol use. They were all exchanging sex for drugs, although only one was actively selling sex. Pearce and colleagues (2002) found that young women dealing with a number of interlinked concerns had reduced control over their lives and that service delivery needs to be able to understand and work with multifaceted problems.

Working with these young women necessitated much more than the simple provision of information about the risks they were running. It required an exploration of their ability to examine the choices they had and the choices they wanted to make. These were not simply about the risk of sexually transmitted diseases, unwanted pregnancies, drug addiction and sexual exploitation, but also about how they wanted to be as adults. All of them wished to be 'normal', to be married, to have children and a good job but they had experienced a wide range of sexual behaviours at an age when they were too young to make an informed choice, or, indeed, even to know that some sexual behaviours were a matter of individual choice, rather than the 'norm'.

> Louise joined the group referred to above at the third session. It was explained to her that she could discuss any issues that she was interested in or were bothering her. "Can we talk about sex?", she asked, following up the worker's affirmative answer with "Have you ever been bummed?".
>
> *To what extent should a social care worker answer personal questions? Should workers make their sexual values explicit? What boundary issues are involved?*

Nusbaum and Rosenfeld (2004) make some helpful distinctions here. They suggest that sharing an experience with the aim of helping a service user is a boundary crossing, whereas sharing it to make the social worker feel better, with no benefit to the service user, is a boundary violation. As the two situations are not always entirely distinct and the temptation could be to avoid the situation altogether to be on the 'safe side', they add that to ignore sexual health questions is excessive distance and, therefore, also a boundary violation. In the example above, therefore, it was necessary for the worker, despite her discomfort, to provide sufficient personal information to make the point that 'bumming' is a relatively common sexual activity, but it is also a matter of individual choice and that it is entirely reasonable for a young woman to say 'no' to such a request.

Social workers may also have concerns about the legality of talking about sexual health matters with vulnerable service users, particularly young people, but these concerns are covered by the Fraser Guidelines. These were drawn up to enable health professionals to provide contraceptive advice and treatment to under-16s, provided the following conditions are met:

- the young person understands the professional's advice;
- the young person is encouraged to inform their parents;
- the young person is likely to begin, or continue having, sexual intercourse with or without contraceptive treatment;
- unless the young person receives contraceptive treatment, their physical or mental health, or both, will suffer;

- the young person's best interests require them to receive contraceptive advice or treatment with or without parental consent.

Similar provision is made in Scotland by the 1991 Age of Legal Capacity (Scotland) Act. Although the criteria in England, Wales and Scotland specifically refer to contraception, the principles apply to other treatments, most notably abortion, although any sexual health risk would apply as long as the advice is in the best interests of the young person. The 2003 Sexual Offences Act (which became law in May 2004) further clarifies matters. It does not alter the way in which health professionals or others working with children and young people can provide sexual health information, advice or treatment. Neither does it prevent the provision of confidential advice and treatment to young people under 16, including those under 13, and a worker does not commit an offence if they act for the purpose of:

- protecting a child from sexually transmitted infection;
- protecting the physical safety of the child;
- preventing the child from becoming pregnant;
- promoting the child's emotional well-being by giving advice.

These exceptions cover not only health professionals but also anyone who acts to protect a child. Those providing treatment without parental consent will continue to assess competence on a case-by-case basis, and at each consultation, and work within the Fraser Guidelines. Confidentiality can only be breached in exceptional circumstances where the health, safety and welfare of the young person or others would otherwise be at grave risk. The decision whether to breach confidentiality depends on the degree of current or likely harm, not solely on the age of the child or young person.

The Act aims to protect young people from abuse and exploitation, not to prosecute mutually agreed sexual activity between young people of a similar age where there is no evidence of exploitation. Thus, although it is illegal for a man or boy over the age of 10 to have sexual intercourse with a young woman aged 13, 14 or 15, this is potentially defensible if he is 23 or under at the time of the offence and has not previously been charged with an offence of this kind. It is an absolute offence for a man or boy aged 10 or over to have sexual intercourse with a girl aged 12 or under; and where sexual exploitation is involved, it remains a child protection issue until the young person reaches the age of 18. Government is considering making it compulsory for GPs and health workers to contact the police if a girl of 13 or under seeks contraceptive advice, as such a girl is not legally able to consent to sexual intercourse, and her partner is therefore committing rape.

> Annie became pregnant to her 16-year-old brother when she was 12 years old. She had a termination and was accommodated by the local authority. She has contact with her mother and 11-year-old brother, Liam, at the children's home. She has been seen with Liam near the family home when she should have been in school.
>
> *What sexual issues would you discuss with Annie? Would you consider it suitable to seek contraceptive provision for Annie and, if so, could you promise her confidentiality? What are the legal requirements that would influence your discussion with Annie?*

For workers talking with young people who are unsure of their sexuality, the same Act legalised homosexual acts between males, provided they are both over 16 (17 in Northern Ireland). There are no offences, other than indecent assault, related to lesbianism; provided both women consent, and neither is under the age of consent, acts of lesbianism are legal.

Talking to service users about sexual health

When talking about sexual health matters, health professionals recommend that the worker be available; answer questions honestly; use correct terms; talk about sex more than once; respect service user privacy; listen carefully; and share their own values. This is easier said than done; even though good communication skills are fundamental to effective social work, raising sexual topics with service users also raises sexual issues for the worker. Like most people, social workers will have experienced some sort of sexual dysfunction at some point in their lives and a substantial number will have been sexually abused, or be in sexually abusive relationships. As the emphasis in talking about sexual topics is on emotional attitudes and the nature of sexual interaction rather than sexual responses (Fraser, 1987), the quality of workers' current relationships also surfaces. This means that raising sexual topics is potentially threatening to workers' own sense of self-esteem. Avoiding the subject altogether is not the only danger in talking about sexual issues; it is also possible that a worker may feel so uncomfortable that issues are raised in an insensitive manner; for example, in the course of a child protection assessment, one young mother was outraged at being asked baldly how many sexual partners she had had. It is important then that workers understand their own sexuality to ensure that they are not liable to difficulties in communicating on sexual issues. Nusbaum and Rosenfeld (2004) provide a list of questions you can ask yourself to increase your understanding:

Sources of sexual information	When you were a child, where did you get most of your information about sexuality?
	How have these sources changed over the years?
Discussion of sexuality in family of origin	How easy was it to discuss issues around sexuality when you were growing up?
	How did the topic of menstruation or wet dreams come up?
	How easy was it to discuss sexuality with your family or friends?
Expression of affection in family of origin	How was affection expressed in your family when you were growing up?
	How has this changed over the years?
	How has expression of affection in your family of origin impacted on your sexuality?
	How often do you touch someone affectionately without it meaning a signal for sexual activity?
Family of origin (religiosity)	Were you raised in a religion?
	How strong was your religious upbringing?
	How has this changed over the years?
	How did religion in your family of origin impact on your discussion of sexuality?

Purpose for sex	As a child, what messages did you receive about the purpose for sex? How has this changed over the years? How do the messages about the purpose of sex impact on sexuality?
Talking about sex	Have you ever wanted to confide in anyone about sexual issues? Have you ever been a service user? Have you ever been asked about your sexual history? Would you have liked to discuss sexual issues at your last health visit?

Vanessa discusses a child protection assessment she is undertaking in supervision. The case involves the sexual abuse of two young children by their father; he has since left the home and Vanessa is assessing the mother's ability to protect. Vanessa discloses that she was sexually abused by her father as a child but was disbelieved by her mother. She says that she has never discussed this with anyone but the experience means that she has a special understanding of the risk to the children and she doubts the mother's ability to protect.

What issues would you expect the supervisor to raise with Vanessa?

Not only do social workers need to understand their own sexuality, but they also have to develop a sexual language that they feel comfortable with, and which the service user can understand. The advice noted above to use correct terms can lead to a stilted conversation with people accustomed to using other terms. When working with young men whose behaviour is sexually concerning or abusive, the authors often use the board game, Man's World, as a means of discussing sexual topics in a relaxed way, and ascertaining the young person's sexual knowledge. As the participants in the game travel round the board, they have to answer four types of questions to gain cards to build a 'complete man': true or false questions; chance questions; 'What if?' questions; and personal questions.

1. *True or false questions*: these are factual assertions to ascertain sexual knowledge, but the wording of them employs both accurate terms

and more commonly used ones; for example, 'One of the testes (balls) hangs lower than the other'. This enables the worker to develop a sexual language that has meaning to the service user. Consulting the answers after each true or false card is answered, whether or not the worker knows the answer, creates an atmosphere where it is okay to admit to knowledge gaps, as well as encouraging further discussion.

2. *Chance questions*: these are a mixture of true and false assertions and more open-ended questions, which again provide opportunities to enlarge the discussion, and language. For example, the question 'What happens when you get an erection?' not only allows further talk about the phenomenon but also establishes what terms are more commonly used: the follow-up question 'What do you and your mates call an erection?' elicits answers such as 'The lads call it a boner but the lasses call it a stiffy'. Quite easily and naturally, all the players are talking comfortably about erections.

3. *'What if?' questions*: these involve dilemmas commonly encountered as part of becoming a man; for example, 'What would you do if your mate told you he was being abused by his dad?', 'What would you do if you found condoms in your girlfriend's handbag?', 'What would you do if your mates asked you to break into a house with them?'. These questions help contextualise both sexual and social behaviour within current relationships.

4. *Personal questions*: there are a number of questions aimed at personal qualities; for example, 'What aspect of your personality would you most like to change?' and 'What do you like most about being a man?'.

Although this game is specifically designed for use with young men, it provides a fun way for all the players to talk about their sexual knowledge and values. Where the young person's carers have joined in, they have enjoyed the game as much as the young person. The sexual ice has been broken, so they are comfortable and confident in their ability to continue talking about sexual issues with the young person as they occur in everyday life. Whether or not you work with young men, it is worth acquiring Man's World and playing the game with colleagues as a fun way of understanding your own sexuality, checking your sexual knowledge and developing your sexual language. Popular magazines are also useful resources; despite a seeming preoccupation with sexual prowess, they are a good source of discussion on sexual relationship dilemmas. Quillam (2005), for example, found that teenage magazines give good information and advice that is well thought through and supports the values of good communication and consent in relationships.

Introducing sexual issues with service users is difficult because social workers may worry that the service user will be offended or embarrassed. There are also special sensitivities, as some sexual activities carry stigma, and all sexual issues raise issues of confidentiality, faith and trust. Curtis et al (1995) suggest using a 'hook' or 'excuse' to introduce the subject:

- As Valentine's Day/the holiday season/Christmas is coming up, do you have any concerns you would like to raise about your relationships and sex life?
- Are you permitted by faith to discuss sexual matters?

The emphasis in talking about sexual topics with service users is on sexuality in relationships; the social worker does not require a detailed knowledge of sexual diseases and sexual responses. This is the province of the sexual health specialist.

Further reading

Nusbaum, M. and Rosenfeld, J.A. (2004) *Sexual Health across the Life Cycle: A Practical Guide for Clinicians*, Cambridge: Cambridge University Press.

Summary

- Promoting sexual health is not just about the prevention of disease and pregnancy; good sexual health is an important part of physical and mental health, which impacts on our identity, relationships and longevity.
- There is a clear relationship between sexual ill health, poverty and social exclusion (high risk of unintended pregnancy, sexually transmitted illnesses, restricted choices and unsatisfactory sexual relationships). Therefore the promotion of sexual health is a key area of social work.
- The Fraser Guidelines and the 2003 Sexual Offences Act provide protection from prosecution to social workers talking to children under the age of consent about sexual issues.
- Social workers need to be comfortable with their own sexuality, check their sexual knowledge and develop a sexual language before talking with service users about such matters.

FIVE

Developing sexual well-being in children and young people

Initiatives aimed at safeguarding the sexual well-being of children proliferated in the 1980s following an increased awareness of the incidence, and damaging effects, of child sexual abuse. Early prevention programmes were targeted at helping children become aware of 'stranger danger' (see, for example, Elliott, 1985) and were considered largely the province of teaching (see, for example, Milner and Blyth, 1989). Since then, sexual safety teaching has been largely incorporated into Personal, Social and Health Education lessons in schools, although keeping safe programmes are often delivered by visiting specialists, as teachers often fear that pupils may make false allegations if they introduce such topics. Government-issued guidance to safeguard teachers (*Responding to Allegations Against Teachers*, DfES, 2004a, and *Safeguarding Children in Education*, DfES, 2004b) establishes the need to make arrangements to take all reasonable measures to ensure that the risk of harm to children and young people is minimised and sets out the need to ensure that induction and follow-up training is provided for all school staff to enable them to fulfil their responsibilities effectively in respect of child protection. The guidance recommends that the management of sexualised behaviour in schools be approached on a whole-school as well as classroom/curriculum and individual level. Thus not only are children taught how to protect themselves but school staff are also trained to recognise and respond to sexualised behaviour.

Nine-year-old Emma has been referred by her school. She is experiencing difficulties at school and her parents find it difficult to get her to attend. She sometimes leaves school at midday. She has previously been reprimanded for playing games with younger children that involve her taking their knickers down. Yesterday she was seen disappearing in to bushes with a male pupil in her class.

What are the issues here? Would you wish to see other children as well as Emma? How would you talk to the children?

Keeping safe work does not necessarily require specialist skills and knowledge as long as the worker is well prepared.

Stage 1. Preparatory work. The social worker will have well-developed skills and resources in working with children and it is useful to remind oneself of these – the games that children enjoy, the books that have proved helpful, and the collection of stickers and soft toys that have been accumulated. Essex (2005) also recommends that the worker practise drawing stick people, chairs, beds and so on, as these skills will be needed when explaining to very young children issues such as whom they need to keep safe from, why the judge will not let a family member come home yet, or safe/unsafe places in the home.

In order to avoid the difficulty of giving children the knowledge of how to keep themselves safe when they lack the power to enact safety strategies, it is important that the work is undertaken in conjunction with either parents or carers. Even where a parent is the abuser, this is not a contraindication, as the child needs to know from whom they need to be safe. In addition, parents and carers are best placed to support the teaching by utilising real-life situations as they occur. For example, one mother with whom we worked followed up privacy rules in the house when she noticed her daughter leaving the toilet door open and explained about appropriate kisses after her daughter invited adults to kiss her goodnight.

Time spent preparing parents or carers before work begins with the child would usefully include:

- identifying the family's sexual language. For example, what terms do they use to describe sexual organs, what do they say when they are going to the toilet and so on. Most families have a word for penis but often do not have words to describe female organs;
- increasing parents' and carers' confidence in their capacity to talk about sexual matters by giving them appropriate reading matter. For example, one parent found the questionnaires about sexual assault in Elliott (1985) useful in increasing her knowledge of sexual assault;
- explaining which topics you will be covering in each session, and asking if parents or carers are willing to join in each session, and whether their children prefer games, drawing or talk. Their participation is an important component of the work. For example, it is better that the person whose duty it is to protect does any drawing round a child's body. Ask parents or carers which materials they already have to use in each session. This will save you from

carrying around a large bag of crayons, paper and so on, as well as contextualising the session within the family's own resources and usual habits.

Stage 2. Safety-building work with the child. There is no set formula for this, other than starting with simple, non-threatening safety issues before moving on to more emotionally charged and complex issues. A typical programme is outlined below:

Establishing the child's right to be safe. Ask the child about basic rights such as breathing, eating, sleeping and going to the toilet, and what would happen if these rights were taken away. Then introduce the idea of the right to feel safe by asking the child for examples of when they feel safe. Before talking about body safety, it is useful to ask about other safety situations, such as does the child know how to keep safe in the home (around scissors and knives, for example), on the road, if lost and so on. As each safety competency is established, this can be written on a cardboard star and blanks given to the child to fill in as they remember other competencies. These can be built up into a safety necklace of stars.

Privacy. A simple way to help a child understand that certain parts of their body are private and personal is to draw round the child's body on a sheet of wallpaper and then ask them to colour in the parts of the body that are covered by their bathing costume. When there is more than one child in the session, it may be appropriate for the children to draw round each other. Where one child has exhibited sexually concerning or harmful behaviour, it is more appropriate for the protective parent or carer to do the drawing. While the child is colouring, questions can be asked about why these body parts are private and who is allowed to touch them, and where. This should lead naturally to discussion about privacy in bedrooms and toilets, and the child can be helped to draw a diagram of the house, marking each room where other people are not allowed to touch them with a cross or scowling face sticker and other rooms with a tick or smiley face sticker. This should lead to further discussion on privacy, such as not coming downstairs undressed, and a list of family privacy rules can be drawn up.

Good and bad touches. Building on the touching discussed during the wallpaper-body drawing, saying 'no' to touches the child dislikes can be introduced. It is easiest to introduce this topic by talking about tickling, horseplay or big hugs, as very few children actually like these, although many parents think that they do. Adults or siblings hearing the child talk about disliking these sorts of touches, agreeing not to do them again, and giving the child permission to say 'no', is an important part of keeping the child safe as well as demonstrating that it is not the child's sole responsibility to keep themselves safe.

Good and bad secrets. The easiest way to introduce this topic is to ask the child about a good secret, most usually a birthday present. Asking for examples of bad secrets may elicit all sorts of answers, including information which parents may not wish to be shared with professionals (the authors accidentally discovered that one mum was a secret binge drinker on one occasion). Although not directly concerned with bad secrets about unwanted sexual touching, these examples provide the opportunity to talk about the difference between gifts and bribes (given to make children do something they do not want to do) and tricks – both of which are commonly used to ensure that the child keeps a bad secret.

Telling adults. As noted earlier, it is difficult for children to say 'no' to powerful or loved people, and neither should they have to take on the burden of being responsible for controlling other people's abusive behaviour. It is easier for the child if they can identify a trusted adult to whom they can turn to for help. Barnardo's The Junction (2005) has developed the idea of identifying a 'helping hand' as a visual reminder of whom the child can turn to if they have a problem, no matter how small or awful it might seem. The child is asked to draw round their hand and nominate the person they would like on their helping hand. The key person's name is written on the thumb of their hand and the other digits used for people who would offer supplementary or different support. It is important that the people nominated are asked if they will offer support and how they can be contacted. At least one person on a child's helping hand can be a pet or a teddy bear, as these can be sources of emotional support while the child works out whether or not to tell.

Stage 3. Problem solving. Even young children can grasp the concepts of sexual safety training but find it difficult to say 'no' or tell. Research shows that they are more likely to act on their knowledge if they have problem-solving skills. In preparation for this session, the child can be given a storybook such as *Super Dooper Jezebel* (by Tony Ross, Anderson Press), which makes the point in a humorous way that over-compliance in children can be dangerous. Elliott (1985) suggests that 'What if?' games are a playful way of improving a child's problem-solving skills. She recommends that the 'What if?' questions start with something simple, like 'What if a monkey came to the door?' and follow this with more general safety questions, such as 'What if you saw smoke coming from the house next door?', before moving on to more sensitive questions, such as 'What if your babysitter asked you to play secret games and offered to let you stay up late?'.

Finalising family rules. The various components of the safety training are now summarised in a set of family rules, although these can also contain items about who washes up, bedtimes and so on. The family rules should be negotiated and agreed by all family members, the child being able to take an active part in this because of their participation in earlier sessions and the experience of being listened to. Children at risk of actual or possible sexual abuse are often passive, and compliant and have low self-esteem, so an important test of an effective outcome of the work will be the child's ability to take part in the formulating of family rules. The child can also be awarded a Safe Care Certificate to celebrate achievements and as a visual reminder of how to keep safe. Barnardo's Keep Safe Project in Liverpool collates all the safety work, along with the artwork, into a personal record for the child. Moreover, there is no reason why parents or carers who have been supportive to the child during the training should not be presented with a Certificate of Competence in Protection from Harm.

Fourteen-year-old Steven was sexually abused by a family friend at the age of seven. Since then, there have been a range of unsubstantiated allegations about his sexually concerning behaviour with boys visiting the home and the school has complained that he makes sexually inappropriate comments to girl pupils. His mother reports that she found him sitting astride his six-year-old sister, Ellie, in the lounge. They were both fully dressed but Ellie has since shown sexualised behaviour.

Prepare a plan of work that enables Ellie to be safe from Steven, and Steven to be safe from allegations.

Children with physical and learning difficulties are especially vulnerable to sexual abuse, as are adults who carers have found to consistently overestimate their charges' abilities to comprehend such issues (Banat et al, 2002). Programmes designed to help this vulnerable population keep safe need to be lengthier to ensure that learning is consolidated and a wider variety of materials for use in such programmes would be helpful: games, role play, photos, video feedback and drawing, for example, all promote learning (Long and Holmes, 2001). Harper and Hopkinson (2002) provide an outline of a protective behaviour programme for people of all ages with learning disabilities; Brown et al (1996) provide a useful manual for working with adults with learning disabilities; and Brewster (2004) explains how to use Talking Mats with children who have limited speech.

Ten-year-old Michael and his nine-year-old sister, Sadie, have been sexually abused by a family friend. They both attend their local junior school, although Michael has a special statement of educational need, since he has been diagnosed with Asperger's syndrome. Sadie is showing similar traits. Michael has a reading age of seven but does not always comprehend what he has read. Sadie has a reading age of five. They are both very eager to please and have no concept of sexual safety.

How would you approach keep safe work with these children? Which materials might be useful?

Reducing teenage sexual risk taking

The sexual well-being of teenagers is more fragile than that of adults, mainly due to their increased, and earlier, sexual activity than previous generations, combined with a wide range of risk-taking behaviours. Most teenagers first have heterosexual intercourse at the age of 16, with a substantial minority reporting an earlier start. By the age of 20, only a very few people will not have had sex (DH, 2001a). As the chance of a sexually active young woman becoming pregnant within a year is 90%, it is no surprise that 16% of all 15- to 16-year-olds do so. Young people are poor contraceptive users and, even when they use a contraceptive method, they have higher failure rates than older women. The experience of abortion or a pregnancy scare does not increase subsequent regular use of reliable contraceptive methods (Fu et al, 1999). Increased sexual activity among young people has also been accompanied by an increase in sexually transmitted infections (STIs): between 1995 and 1997, 16- to 19-year-olds had the highest rate of increase in gonorrhoea, and diagnoses for chlamydia rose by 5%; 20-30% of young women diagnosed with an STI have another within 18 months (SEU, 1999). Hooker and Wallace (2000) estimate that one third of all STIs occur in young people. Risks associated with STIs are increased in young people, as they tend to present late for treatment (Lindsay, 2001).

These risks to sexual well-being are compounded by other health risks: more than 40% of all 16-year-olds report that they drink weekly and indulge in binge drinking, and the use of drugs increases to 30% of all 14- to 15-year-olds and 37% of 15- to 16-year-olds (Walker et al, 1999). These behaviours also concern the young people themselves; Bekaert (2005) links them to increased suicide, depression and self-harm rates to illustrate that young people's sexual and allied activity is detrimental to their health both in the short and long term.

The government's response has been to increase information to prevent poor sexual health, and to improve services offering contraceptive care, abortion and the diagnosis and treatment of STIs (DH, 2001a). To this end, there has been an emphasis on more effective sex and relationship education in schools, and the provision of one-stop sexual health clinics. It might seem, then, that social workers do not need to concern themselves with the sexual well-being of their service users but neither improved information nor diagnosis and treatment will be sufficient to improve the sexual well-being of young people generally, and the disadvantaged (who make up the majority of social workers' teenage service users) specifically. Young people will remain at risk of unwanted teenage pregnancy and STIs not because they are simply reckless and ignore advice and treatment opportunities but because they are not always able to act on that advice or access treatment.

Young people generally are limited in their ability to make rational, informed decisions about how to act on their sexual desires because they lack a repertoire of behaviours. Early teenage boys have, on average, four erections a night and by 17 at least two thirds have at least one wet dream a month (Tomlinson, 1999). Young men do not necessarily talk to each other about this in a helpful way; one young person told the authors in a counselling session that his first wet dream scared him, as he did not know what was happening. Young men's peer conversations tend to be of a boastful nature, and more influenced by pornography than sex and relationship education in schools. Thus it is not surprising that early male sexual activity is characterised by spontaneous action and curiosity. Much less is known about female sexual desire (Parsons, 1999) but young women's interest in sexual activity is likely to be heavily influenced by men's pressures on them to engage in sex, having their bodies commented on negatively by young men, and risking their reputations to avoid the fear of rejection in their early other-sex relationships. Where these men are young, they are also opportunistic and ignorant; where they are older, they are often predatory.

The dilemmas for young women are compounded by the complex interaction of various risk factors. For example, increased female contraception use may reduce the risk of unwanted pregnancy but it is linked with an increased vulnerability to STIs. The increased use of drugs and alcohol also interacts with sexual well-being; a survey by the Health Education Authority (1998) found that one in five of the young people interviewed about sex and intoxication had had sex they later regretted; one in seven had had unsafe sex; and one in 10 had been unable to remember whether they had had sex the night before.

> Chloe (15 years old) and Rosie (14 years old) are the only two girls in a six-bedded children's home. They have built up a close friendship and spend each Saturday shopping and hanging around with older lads. They have been coming home later and later from these outings and, last weekend, they were deposited by an irate taxi driver who reported that they had hired him outside a pub in the centre of town. The girls had refused to pay him and were so drunk they had been sick in his cab.
>
> *What practical steps would you take at this point? What sexual issues would you discuss with Chloe and Rosie the next day? How might their sexual well-being be promoted in the longer term?*

The majority of sexual health services for young people provide advice and treatment on contraception, abortion and pregnancy. Thus they are aimed primarily at young women. This not only places an unrealistic burden of responsibility on to young women to manage men's sexuality, but also means that men are excluded from service provision. The result of this is that they are also excluded from decision making at all levels. For example, social workers are much more likely to discuss the pros and cons of the contraceptive pill with a sexually active young woman service user than they are to discuss condom use with a young man. Bekaert (2005) suggests that young men who are not encouraged to take decisions about fertility control are likely to withdraw from taking responsibility for contraception and sexual health issues in a relationship. Similarly, when the relationship breaks down but he subsequently becomes a young father, the same young man is likely to be denied access to his child. While this focuses attention on the urgent needs of the young mother, it ignores the fact that young men often want to stay in touch with their children and play a part in their upbringing (Corylon and McGuire, 1999). Being marginalised in decision making about sexual health matters means that young men have little opportunity to increase their emotional literacy and little incentive to desist from high–risk-taking behaviours.

> Eighteen-year-old Chris has attempted suicide following the break-up of his relationship with 16-year-old Emma. They have had a stormy relationship for two years but always got back together after what were increasingly violent rows over both of them being unfaithful. Emma finally decided to break from Chris when she became pregnant and he knocked her to the ground. He is distraught that she will not see him again and that she has told him that she will not allow him to see the baby when it is born.
>
> *What are the sexual and relationship issues that are relevant to Chris in both the short and long term?*

Social workers are most likely to be working with young people who are marginalised, and these are the young people whose sexual well-being is most at risk. Poverty is linked with increased risk of teenage pregnancy and STIs, with disenfranchised young people being most vulnerable because of a lack of positive role models within the home from which they can learn about healthy relationships. Frequent moves, truancy and school exclusion mean that they miss out on sex and relationship education, and are vulnerable to abuse when looking for love. The research into children in care shows that both during and after care the likelihood of being a teenage parent is 25% higher than for young people living with parents, with one quarter of care leavers having a child by 16 and almost half of young women becoming mothers within two years of leaving care (Biehal et al, 1992, 1995). Similarly, young people in care are highly likely to be sexually abused by an adult or peer while in care (Sinclair and Gibbs, 1998), especially those who are disabled.

Prostitution/commercial child sex abuse

Marginalised young people are also particularly at risk of entering prostitution (Barnardo's, 1998; Milner et al, 2002). Pearce et al (2002) identified 26 factors linked to increased risk of being involved in prostitution:

- history of intermittent truanting;
- regular (at least weekly) binge drinking of alcohol;
- history of going missing or running away;
- history of familial physical abuse;
- school non-attender;
- sexual health problems;
- has boyfriend who is physically violent;
- has been in care or looked after;
- has a boyfriend at least four years older than themselves;
- self-harms;
- regular (at least weekly) heroin use;
- history of familial sexual abuse;
- works for boyfriend (selling sex for money for boyfriend or selling or swapping sex for drugs);
- has been raped;
- has a police record;
- is homeless;
- has attempted suicide;
- has been abducted for at least two nights;
- has been abducted by boyfriend;
- has been known to have bullied others at school;
- has been pregnant;
- has worked with police to press charges against abuser;
- has had a baby;
- has diagnosed learning difficulties;
- has diagnosed mental health problems;
- has been in prison.

Pearce found that the most common issues shared by the majority of the young women in her study (55) were truanting from school or not being on a school roll; regular (at least weekly) binge drinking of alcohol; having a history of going missing or running away from home or care; having experience of familial physical abuse; having had sexual health problems and boyfriends who are physically violent towards them; and having been in care or looked after by the local authority. Although none of these factors, or any particular combination, directly causes young women to enter prostitution, they indicate the number of complex problems the young women were facing at any one time. Young women with such difficulties who are living in care are exposed to peers who introduce them to prostitution (for an overview, see Cusik, 2002). Male teenage prostitution is also associated with marginalisation, especially drug use (Leichtentritt and Arad, 2005).

Bluett et al (2000) estimate that in any one year there are 2,000 young people involved in prostitution in the UK, with one third of them aged under 16. Most adult prostitutes were under age when they first started (Skidmore, 2000; Gillies et al, 2004). They were also mostly vulnerable young people already in contact with welfare services (Cusik and Martin, 2003), so could have been prevented from being drawn into prostitution had effective exiting services been available, such as the Nottingham Prostitute Outreach Workers service to children's care homes (Gillies et al, 2004). The Cusik and Martin study shows that most local authorities lack a coherent policy for dealing with teenage prostitution but there is much that social workers can do to prevent young people from becoming trapped in prostitution. Naming the activity is an important starting point; there is a tendency to refer to prostitution as 'sex work', but this implies a choice that rarely exists for vulnerable young people. No one aspires to become a prostitute; it is not something a person can put on a passport or CV: 'The sex markets we have examined were not, in the main, staffed by "happy hookers". Most of them disliked the work intensely, and felt coerced into it by drug dependence, poverty or pimps' (May et al, 1999, p 38).

The damaging effects of prostitution on young people's lives are well documented. Swann (1998) lists extreme physical, sexual and emotional abuse at the hands of pimps, including broken bones and burns, rapes and sexual assaults leading to sexually transmitted diseases, self-mutilation, overdosing, eating disorders and drug addiction. In their overview of the research, Lenihan and Dean (2000) emphasise poverty, rejection and chaotic lives as consequences, and Barrett (1997, p 163) lists violence, invisibility, denial, harassment, ghettoisation and health risks.

That drug use plays a part in maintaining young people in prostitution is evident in much of the research, with sex markets playing a significant role in the development of drug markets and vice versa (May et al, 1999; Cusik and Martin, 2003). Children in the care system are particularly vulnerable to being recruited into prostitution, as they meet all the criteria for entry identified in the research. Kelly et al (1995) report that most basic rehabilitation schemes have a low rate of success, possibly because the young people's perceptions of themselves and life have changed in complex ways, making it difficult ever to return to an 'ordinary' life. However, Cusik and Martin found that the most important factor in assisting a young person's exit from prostitution was reducing drug dependence, and the most important factors in preventing young people from being drawn into prostitution were identifying vulnerable young people and ensuring that they are securely housed, socially included and have access to services on the basis of need (p 43). They also recommend pursuing and prosecuting child abusers who pay to have sex with children; increased use of Section 47 child protection assessments could be a means of targeting the weakest link in the drugs/prostitution market. The possibility of a man not being allowed to live with his own children may be effective in reducing prostitution use, as may sending letters and postcards to the registered owners of cars observed kerb-crawling. Equally, the legislation on abduction can be used where an older man is living with a young person who may be too fearful of the offender or has been groomed not to give evidence of under-age sexual activity.

As well as being required to initiate child protection procedures for young people involved in prostitution, as guidance states that these young people are to be treated as victims of abuse (DH, 2001c), social workers have specific duties in respect of the most complex problems affecting sexual well-being. For example, government guidance places a duty on them to provide young people in care with the knowledge and skills they require for positive sexual relationships (DH, 2001b). Social workers also have a professional duty to use their expertise to improve the sexual well-being of all young people with whom they work. Some countries have similar social class variations, educational levels and areas of poverty to the UK but not the same high levels of teenage pregnancy; the main difference is an open and accepting attitude in these other countries to teenage sexuality, including a willingness to talk about sex, raise a person's self-esteem and encourage their ambitions and life hopes (Bekaert, 2005). Where teenage sexuality is the subject of adult moralising, such as the abstention campaign in the US, teenage pregnancy rates are unaffected, so it seems obvious that didactic education will be ineffective. As Couzens (1999) says about group work with young people, 'it's pretty hard to have an interesting conversation if everything is negative' (p 26).

How to talk to young people about sex, drugs and alcohol needs thoughtfulness but is not really all that difficult if such conversations are embedded in young people's ambitions and life hopes: all the studies of high-risk behaviours indicate that young people hope to have a happy and fulfilling intimate relationship. For example, we have found when talking to young gay men that it is not necessary to lecture them on the sexual risks associated with anal intercourse; this is as much a matter of concern for heterosexual young people – about one third of whom are thought to use anal sex occasionally, with about 10% using it as a regular method (Wellings et al, 1994). When listened to about their concerns, these are usually associated with wanting a cuddle and resentment at having to wait until they are 16 before this is legal, something that it is hard to bear when their heterosexual friends are making dates with girlfriends and boyfriends at a much earlier age. And it is unwise to assume that a young person's sexuality is fixed:

> Many young people will be having sex with their own gender, but may define themselves as either hetero-, homo- or bisexual, and this may have little bearing on how they self-identify later in life. Some young people with no same sexual experience will still identify as lesbian, gay or bisexual. (Davies, 1999a)

Ivan lives with foster parents in a small village which has a strongly macho culture. In a year 10 PSHE lesson, he announced that he was gay. His best friend has since shunned him and his head of year is worried that he may make overtures to other boys. His foster mother took his mobile phone from him after discovering that he was receiving texts from older gay men. Ivan is totally perplexed with the 'fuss', as he says 'Shona came out last year and no one said a word'.

What issues would you discuss with Ivan? To what extent do you share the head of year's and foster mother's concerns?

Neither is it accurate to presume that lesbian young women are safe from STIs; there is tremendous diversity in the choice of sexual partner, what they do together, what they mean to each other, and the impact on their health. Although sexual *activity* between women is relatively safe, lesbian *identity* does not offer protection against the conditions associated with heterosexual sexual activity (Wilton, 2000). And lesbian young women have added risks, as they tend not to access gynaecology or contraceptive clinics and therefore do not get screened (Gruskin, 1999).

It is also unwise to consider that disabled young people's sexual health is not at risk simply because they may not be able to engage in sexual intercourse. Middleton (1999) found that the disabled young people in her study were sexually active but had not been able to talk about their worries; disability being about tragedy and passivity meant that they received conflicting messages from adults about risk and sexual activity. This also made them more vulnerable to abuse.

Blackburn's (2002) study of young people with spina bifida and hydrocephalus contained at least one person who was HIV positive.

Talking to young people

The simplest way of introducing sex into a conversation with a young person is to ask them a series of scaled questions, starting with a general self-esteem question, such as 'On a scale of 1-100, if 100 is the best you could possibly feel about yourself, where are you on this scale today?'. As self-esteem is a complex concept and varies depending on context, follow-up questions could include:

- If you were one point higher, what would be different?
- If 1 means you hate your body and 10 means you are completely happy with the way you look, where are you on this scale today?
- If 1 is the pits and 10 means that you could not be happier, where are you on this scale today?
- If 1 means you are very unhappy in your relationship and 10 means you are blissfully happy, where are you on this scale today?

Depending on the young person's answers, follow-up questions would address issues to do with accuracy of sexual knowledge, how much a young person is being coerced into sexual activity either before they are ready or of a nature they do not really enjoy, and how confident they are about contraceptive use. Talking about drugs and alcohol can usefully be addressed through concern for the young person's safety. For example, 'You say that you go out with friends for a drink at the weekend. How do you keep yourself safe?'. Safety in these instances can include questions about friends looking out for one another, getting into cars when intoxicated, how the young person gets home safely, how the young person guards against spiked drinks, and managing money as well as more direct questions about sex, such as 'Have you ever regretted having sex when you were drunk?'. As many troubled young people persist with unsuitable relationships because they offer some sort of love, it is important to ask questions about how the partner shows them respect. These questions are posed from a position of curiosity to facilitate the young person's ability to reflect on the quality of their relationships and begin to recognise their rights and make informed decisions rather than simply exhorting them to stop doing something – be that having sex, using drugs or alcohol, or seeing an exploitative or violent partner.

It is not necessary for the social worker to have an extensive knowledge of the symptoms and treatment of STIs, or know about all the available contraceptive methods, or all forms of sexual activity. Health professionals have already carefully considered how to present this information to young people in a form that is both accessible and user-friendly. All the social worker needs to do is equip themselves with a stock of Family Planning Association publications that have been designed specially for young people or give the young person details of a website to look up the information themselves. Some examples of helpful websites are:

- www.feelconfident.co.uk/how_to_put_on_a_condom.htm;
- www.lovelife.uk.com (a website advising on STIs and how to avoid them);
- www.likeitis.org.uk (information about all aspects of sex education and teenage life, including teenage pregnancy, help and advice, periods, lovebugs (STIs), sex, peer pressure, sexuality and contraception);
- www.avert.org/ypbooks.htm (a downloadable leaflet featuring accounts from young men addressing all aspects of gay sexuality).

As websites are frequently updated or removed, it could be even more fruitful to ask a young person to use their computer skills in making a search for the information required.

Peer pressure is often considered as something negative to be counteracted but it is entirely understandable that young people's sexuality will be influenced by their peers; sex, drugs, alcohol and relationships are the main topics of their conversations. But the peer group can become a positive influence and source of constructive support if the social worker is willing and confident to undertake group work. Whatever the initial reason for the formation of a group, whether it be to tackle juvenile offending, improve self-esteem or reduce challenging behaviour, sessions on making choices and decisions about sexual activity will be relevant to the group. Bekaert (2002) provides a useful list of questions for such a session:

- What are we looking for in a relationship?
- When is the right time to have sex?
- How do we talk to the person we are with about sex?
- How do we make positive decisions about whom we have sex with?
- What do we do if we fancy someone?
- How do we know if someone fancies us?

- How should we act?
- What is appropriate?
- What should we do if we feel uncomfortable with, or dislike, what is happening?
- How do our cultural beliefs and values affect our choices and decisions in relationships?
- What is sexuality?
- Whom are we attracted to, and why?
- How do we talk about and feel comfortable with our sexuality?
- How do we get the best out of relationships and where can we get more information?

With small groups, scaled questions can be used in a circular way. For example, the questions listed above can be written on a flip chart and each group member asked to score themselves. The person with the highest score is then asked 'How do you do that?' as a means of validating young people's knowledge rather than the group facilitator supplying all the information. Then the group can be asked to advise the person with the lowest score. Young people discussing sex, relationships and drugs and alcohol can become very rowdy, partly due to embarrassment and partly due to showing off, so it is useful to have a fun method of enabling the young people to keep themselves on track. Couzens (1999) uses the idea of a football bench in his group work with young men. At each session one group member is the designated referee. If a young person breaks one of the ground rules established by the group, that person is given a warning. For a second breaking of the rules, the young person is sent off – to the bench or sin bin for 10 minutes or so. The group decides the time. When the person comes back into the group, they apologise, then talk about what happened. A third breaking of the rules involves suspension and individual sessions, although Couzens says this rarely happens as a team game feeling develops and works fantastically. Young women are less likely to respond to team rules, and we find that disruptive group members respond well to being asked to make everyone a cup of tea or coffee as this gives them the opportunity to calm down, and be helpful.

No group-work sessions can ignore the importance of mobile phones in young people's lives. Mobile phones are both hazardous to young people and a potential source of support. Pearce et al (2002, p 39) found that their extensive use increased contact with older, exploitative men in her study of young women involved in prostitution, but that they were also a resource that enabled the young women to communicate with friends and those who offer help. Tolerating young people making and receiving calls on their mobiles during group-work sessions facilitates constructive group discussion about the nature of some of the calls. For example, a young person taking a call from an older man will be more confident about refusing an unreasonable request when supported by the group. Similarly, group members can consult with other young people about issues raised in the group. It is also a means of including members who may have missed a session, and enables the group facilitator to raise issues about pornography on mobile phones, especially in young men's groups.

Further reading

Bekaert, S. (2005) *Adolescence and Sex. The Handbook for Professionals Working with Young People*, Abingdon: Radcliffe Publishing Limited.

Summary

- Young children benefit more from keeping safe work when their carers are involved, as this provides them with opportunities to practise concepts learned.
- Children with disabilities require lengthier keep safe programmes that have been specially tailored to their learning needs.
- The sexual health of young people is more fragile than that of adults because of their risk-taking behaviours over a wide range of activities. An open attitude to teenager sexuality and a willingness to talk about sexual issues within the context of a young person's ambitions and life hopes is most effective in promoting good sexual health.
- Young people's sexual identities are fluid and it is not safe to assume that older people of whatever sexual orientation are relatively safe from sexually transmitted illnesses.

SIX

Developing sexual well-being in adults in vulnerable situations

Talking to adults about sexuality is not usually high on the social work agenda, except where the issue is problem sex. This chapter suggests situations where social workers may be inhibited about discussing sex and sexuality with adult service users, and also circumstances where social workers raise issues of sex and sexuality perhaps inappropriately. How adult sexuality becomes the focus of social work assessments is discussed, using a range of vulnerable situations in which adults come into contact with social workers.

Parents and sexuality

The link between parenting and sexuality is so evident that, apart from the odd query from young children about where babies come from, sexual activity is rarely talked about with parents. This is despite the difficulties in adapting to changing nuances of sexual activity: the shift from romance, excitement and experimentation (which is explicitly sexual), to domesticity and parenting (which becomes implicitly non-sexual). When a child is lost, whether through stillbirth, sudden infant death, accident, illness, murder or adoption, the effect of the subsequent grief on sexuality is well documented in the social work literature. For example, Murray Parkes (1986) noted that sexuality diminishes for many people in the early stages of grief, although Swigar et al (1976) found that some people's need for someone to cling on to might lead to increased sexual activity. Losing a child is so awful an event that a tendency to deny the fact by replacement pregnancies has been noted for many years (see, for example, Lewis, 1976), and can interrupt grieving to such an extent that shadow grief plagues some parents for the rest of their lives. This is as true for birth fathers after adoption as for birth mothers (Clapton, 2001; Witney, 2004). In these tragic instances, social workers seem confident about their role, offering grief counselling over extended periods. The loss of a child is not only a matter of personal grief: 'Children take on great symbolic importance in terms of generativity and hope for the future. All parents have hopes and dreams about their children's futures; when a child dies, the hopes and dreams die too' (Osterhuis et al, 1984, p 76).

The significance of children to parents' sense of identity is well documented in the literature on infertility (see, for example, Mason, 1993; Lasker and Borg, 1994; Mack and Tucker, 1996). Both male and female parents not only experience a threat to their possibility of becoming parents but their sexual activity is also affected in two main ways. Sexual problems may be caused or exacerbated by the experience of infertility treatment, or they may be a contributory factor in childlessness. Accepting that one partner is infertile is stressful in itself and its solution, assisted conception, adds to stress. Many couples find the rigours of infertility treatment embarrassing, and sometimes painful. Following the regime prescribed is important to a successful outcome and this can create other stresses. These accumulating stresses affect sexual activity, something that should be a spontaneous and private expression of love and affection. The couple can become obsessively focused on the procreative aspects of sexual activity at the expense of recreational aspects, so it is not difficult for the social worker to recognise the need to discuss sexual issues with couples undergoing infertility treatment. Similarly, where a couple has to come to terms with failed infertility treatment or a person has suffered a miscarriage, talking about sexual issues is clearly on the agenda.

> Janine suffered a miscarriage 11 months ago. She attends the hospital support group, which her husband refers to as 'the weepers'. She has been referred to you by the infertility consultant, as she is due to begin her second round of infertility treatment but he fears that her psychological state is too fragile for this to be successful. She asks you how any kind of conversation can help.
>
> *How do you answer her question? What sexual issues will you raise with her?*

In all these instances, the 'child' is no longer present, a fact that enables a flow of sympathy to be focused on the parents; or, as in unwanted teenage pregnancy, the father is sidelined so that the mother can be viewed as deserving of sympathy and support. It is likely in these instances that the relationship between the bereaved adult and the social worker will be sufficiently empathic for the bereaved adult to raise issues to do with sexuality, even if the social worker forgets to ask about them.

Where parents suffer loss of parenthood, either through a failed adoption application or care proceedings following a child protection investigation, the child remains a living reality whose rights and needs predominate. This means that parents' rights and needs often come a very poor second to those of the child. This is particularly obvious to parents experiencing a child protection investigation; they find that the social worker who was working with them suddenly becomes the child's social worker. Where their child has been placed with grandparents, they lose not only the support of a social worker but possibly also that of their parents. Here we outline some of the sexual issues for parents who are not only losing actual children but also the identity of parenthood. Paradoxically, where social workers are responsible for assessing parental capacity, sexuality can be both inappropriately over- or under-examined.

Lesbian and gay prospective adoptive parents

In the authors' experience, when people are asked what their best hopes are for therapy, they usually reply 'to be normal'. As we saw with the young women discussed earlier, 'being normal' means having friends, an intimate partner, satisfying work and hopes of a comfortable home with children. People have these hopes whether they are hetero- or homosexual; the desire to have children is independent of sexual orientation (Ratigan, 1999). Hicks and McDermott (1999) found that the decision on the part of lesbian and gay couples to adopt:

> … came out of a process of settling down in their lives, relationships becoming established, work and home lives feeling secure and the question of 'starting a family' arising as it does for some people when they reach a settled plateau in their twenties and thirties. (p 149)

Other than sexual identity, the main difference between lesbian/gay and heterosexual prospective adopters is that adoption is likely to be a first choice for the former. This, say Hicks and McDermott, makes prospective lesbian and gay adopters a primary pool for recruitment but one that is ignored in the prevailing social consensus about suitable parents. Although there is no evidence that children parented by lesbian or gay couples thrive any less well than children in more orthodox families (for an overview, see Hargarden and Llewellin, 1999; Hicks, 2005b), notions about the unsuitability of lesbian/gay couples' ability to provide children with appropriate gender roles influence the assessment process. Lesbian and gay adopters' experience of assessment is one of intrusive and unnecessary interest in their lifestyle, 'focusing on their sexuality above all else' (Hicks and McDermott, 1999, p 173). This is not only discriminatory, but also neglects the strengths that lesbian and gay parents have to offer.

Interestingly, where a lesbian or gay person applies to adopt as a single person, they are questioned less about their sexuality, although single male adopters are 'made to feel disadvantaged as their caring skills are denied because of stereotypical views of gender roles' (Owen, 1999a, p 254). In some ways, successful single and lesbian/gay adopters are alike: both groups of parents are more likely to have damaged and/or disabled children placed with them (Owen, 1999b). Single adoptive mothers frequently offer backgrounds in health, education and social care issues that enhance their status and expertise in childcare. This is something that could equally be considered with lesbian and gay couples but is obscured by an overemphasis on their sexuality. Unlike assessments of lesbian and gay prospective adopters, those of single adopters do not focus on sexuality at all. Their sexuality tends to be ignored, ascribing them a 'de-sexed sex-role, rather like the "spinster adopters" of the first World War' (Owen, 1999b, p 257). De-sexing single adopters appears to enable social workers to identify the particular strengths of this group and meet their needs. In their guide to making good assessments in preparation for permanency, Barker et al (2002, p 72) list these as follows:

Potential strengths of single carers:

- non-stigmatising (one quarter of all UK families)
- lack of contradictory adult expectations for the child
- simpler dynamics/negotiation for parent–child relationship
- feeling of safety regarding previous abuse (female carers)

Needs of single carers:

- positive recruitment and clear messages
- to be helped to not feel 'less eligible'
- assessment focused on parenting potential, not on single carer status
- recognition of experience of infertility
- to have their particular strengths clearly identified/ acknowledged
- identification of full potential as carers for a range of children

The sexuality of the child to be adopted is also ignored in assessments preoccupied with 'suitable gender role models'. Although it is difficult to estimate the incidence of same-sex desire in adolescence, a sizeable percentage of all children placed for adoption identify themselves as lesbian or gay (Davies and Neal, 1999b) and many experience difficulties in heterosexual families. As Davies (1999) comments on young people 'coming out', parents' reactions vary and 'acceptance' does not necessarily mean that the young person's sexuality is affirmed or celebrated.

James is a 34-year-old GP in a city centre practice. Simon is a 35-year-old social worker in charge of a youth offending team in the same city. They have been together for 14 years and are currently living in a large Victorian house in a leafy suburb of the city. They have been 'out' socially for many years but James is not 'out' at work. They have three godsons and a number of nieces and nephews who visit regularly and they have now decided that they would like to adopt. They have put themselves forward as prospective adoptive parents for a teenage girl.

Using the good assessment guidance above, prepare for your first visit to James and Simon. What information will you provide? What questions will you ask? In what ways would your questions differ if either, or both, James or Simon were female?

The Lesbian and Gay Foster and Adoptive Parents' Network can be accessed through lagfapn@hotmail.com. Information can also be found on www.positiveparentingcampaign.freeservers.com and www.pinkparents.org.uk.

Parents undergoing a child protection assessment

The fragility of sexual activity when the self-esteem of parents is threatened by the actual or potential loss of a child has already been noted. This is particularly so where parents are at risk of losing a child through their own behaviour. Many couples will find comfort in increased sexual activity but the authors' experience is that as many are likely to experience a reduction in sexual activity. Both men and women talk about it 'not feeling right' to want sex while their children are in care. This feeling seems to some degree related to an emphasis on the parental role; as with parents of very ill children, they feel they have no right to enjoy themselves when their child is in danger (Frank and Maguire, 1988). In one case experienced by the authors, a mother said: 'I'm concentrating on getting my kids back, I'll think about me later'. Parents talk movingly about what they describe as the pain of the 'empty pram': the anguish of seeing children the same age as their own out happily with parents; avoiding visits to relatives and friends who have children; the tears that come when shops fill up with Easter or Christmas goods; and the agony of going into a child's empty bedroom.

Where only one parent loses sexual desire, this can create problems in the couple's relationship. Most obviously, this means that they lose established ways of supporting each other lovingly at a time when it is important that they work together. Insensitive questioning about past sexual activity, which relates to an earlier sexual identity, neglects the reality that many couples have shifted to a parentally focused sexual identity. This makes it hard for parents to accept that their past sexual identity means that they are putting their needs before those of their children, especially as the shift to a parental sexual identity may have been brought home suddenly and painfully by a child's removal. Other misunderstandings occur when the social worker fails to explore the reality of current sexual activity. Booth and Booth (2004) comment that practice wisdom among social workers is that families will continue to have children until they are allowed to keep one, so the presumption is that sexual activity will be continuing. Not only is this inaccurate in most instances but it also leads to over-intrusive sexual monitoring. For example, one young mother who had put on weight after her children had been taken into care was asked by the assessing social worker if she was pregnant. She explained that she had been comfort eating but was still required to take a pregnancy test, adding humiliation to intrusiveness. Had current sexual issues been discussed, concerns about her putting her needs before those of her children would have been easily answered.

Talking about sex with parents during a child protection assessment can be facilitated by simply asking about all facets of the current couple relationship – romantic, domestic and parental. Where sexual activity has reduced because of threats to the parental relationship, social workers can help matters by allowing the couple to demonstrate parental capacity, even though they do not have the day-to-day care of their children. For example, they can ensure that the parents are consulted about their children's likes and dislikes, and that the children wear clothes brought by the parents on contact, and encourage communication between foster and birth parents by means of a diary. It is also important that they avoid making parents feel worthless by asking them to take their children for pre-adoption medicals before the assessment process is completed.

> Kirsty's two pre-school children were taken into care following her starting a relationship with Zaffir. Zaffir is suspected of hitting Kirsty and he has entertained drug-using friends in the home. At the third assessment session, Kirsty breaks into tears, saying: 'I didn't know what people meant when they said they feel empty. But I do now. I woke in the night and heard the kids calling me. I knew they weren't in their bedroom but I had to get up and check. I feel empty'.
>
> *How does this influence your assessment? What questions would you ask her about her sexual relationship with Zaffir?*

Where the assessment process ends with children being permanently removed, the parents' sense of grief will be even greater. As Booth and Booth (1994) point out, however, parents rarely, if ever, receive any help with the emotionally crippling consequences of guilt and grief that can subsequently blight their lives, mar their marital and family relationships and impact on their social functioning and mental health.

Talking to disabled people

As we all know from the last time we had a heavy cold, discomfort, pain or the fear of pain all inhibit sexual desire and function. At times of stress, along with appetite, sexual activity is the first physical function to shut down, although short periods of ill health do not usually impair overall psychological well-being. Longer periods of ill health threaten the psychological and sexual well-being of disabled and chronically ill people as much as their physical health needs. The role of the social worker in promoting the sexual health of this population is largely one of being sensitive to their emotional needs.

A major concern for disabled and ill people is their body image. Once a person's body has 'let them down', it is hard for that person to trust their body. In the authors' own experience, one man said he was unable to share the surgical team's enthusiasm for his successful kidney transplant because his first thoughts every morning were that he had to do 'a body MOT, check that it's still working'. Similarly, a woman who had had extensive surgery for cancer reported that she now saw her body as her enemy. It is not only an issue of the physical body: the appliances that aim to improve a disabled person's life tend to be cold, angular and ugly. Learning to accept them as well as their own bodily shortcomings can be very hard. The professional challenge is to encourage disabled people to develop an attitude towards their body that is realistic to their experience, without launching into 'let's learn to love our bodies' or ignoring the issue altogether. This takes time and patience. Thomas (1999) quotes Sarah, aged 50, on her response to societal emphases on appearance, dancing and the ability to attract partners at social events. She has no disabled friends by choice because it is too much like looking into a mirror:

> I have come a long way on this but expect it will be a life's work to fully accept my appearance ... I know about inner beauty, about beauty in the eye of the beholder, I can even affirm my own beauty. But if you ask about image, many disabled people feel the full negative weight of our society's notions of what is acceptable appearance which can wound deeply. (pp 50–1)

The reality of these experiences needs to be acknowledged. It is not sufficient to bundle disabled people together and think that they will be able to meet each other's needs. Indeed, grouping disabled people together socially can compound disability. Knight (1981) makes the point that 'one disabled person is a disabled person, two disabled people are a field trip, and three disabled people are a rehabilitation centre' (pp 9–10).

The lack of privacy and independence in many disabled people's daily lives can also affect their sexual well-being in that it denies them opportunities. This is especially true of young disabled people who may miss out on ordinary adolescent sexual experience; Middleton (1999) found that young disabled women, in particular, did not seem to have any role models. Blackburn (2002) interviewed 100 young adults with spina bifida and hydrocephalus and found that they lacked appropriate sex education. Four fifths of her sample said that she was the first person with whom they had discussed sexual concerns, such as how their disability might affect potency; whether they could get pregnant and, if so, whether they could have a normal birth; and how to use contraception, for example, how to use a condom when they were wearing a penile sheath. These young people had received some sex education, but the materials used all had shown beautiful, able-bodied, white subjects. A combination of lack of sex education and physical dependence in this group also demonstrated the vulnerability of disabled people to sexual abuse; the qualitative interview group disclosed physical, sexual and emotional abuse, with two cases ongoing.

These young people also worried about continence management, a hidden impairment that affects the sexual confidence of many disabled people, such as those with multiple sclerosis (Silcock, 2003).

> Graham is a young man in a residential care home for people with muscular dystrophy. His condition has deteriorated to the extent that he is confined to bed. He tells you that he does not want to die a virgin.
>
> *How would you respond to Graham?*

However, no single approach is appropriate to the sexual well-being of disabled people. Much depends on the stage in the lifecycle at which disability occurs. The degree of adjustment may be no different but the process could be. As we have seen above, early impairment affects social and sexual confidence – although not sexual risk taking. Later impairment is more likely to be an issue of loss. The degree of grief attached to the loss will depend on the importance of sexual function for each individual; sexual impairment may be deeply resented and involve a collapse in self-worth, or it may be regarded as trivial. A sudden dependence on a partner can also affect sexual functioning adversely. Where the person's condition is a deteriorating one, both the service user's and carer's sexual needs require regular reassessment. Clausen et al (2005) make the point that advances in palliative care treatment mean that while there are many more disabled people living in the community, their carers' needs are neglected.

It is not necessary for social workers to have a detailed knowledge of the specific problems associated with different types of illness and disability, the effects of drugs, or the sex aids available. If necessary, such information can be obtained from SPOD, 286 Camden Road, London N7 0BJ (0207 607 8851). Practical help would usefully include increasing independence and privacy to increase a disabled person's opportunities to engage in sexual activity, but most important of all is the provision of emotional care. This, says Nichols (2003), does not require specialist counselling skills; it is more appropriately provided as part of a care routine, blended into the overall care plan. It is about giving people an opportunity to identify, express and progress with the normal emotional processes evoked by the situation. It is relevant whether the person is in distress or the impairment is recent. As we saw above, a person may have been disabled for a very long time but never had the opportunity to talk about their sexual health needs. Curtis et al (1995) suggest that the key tasks are to:

- recognise a disabled person's sexuality;
- advise on practical issues, where appropriate;
- support and encourage a disabled person's own solutions.

Special issues for disabled women

Josie, a single woman and newly qualified social care worker, is making an initial visit to Margaret, a 53-year-old single woman. Margaret has been severely disabled all her life but a recent deterioration in her health now means that she has to use a wheelchair.

What knowledge of disability would Josie expect to have? What are the challenges facing Margaret? Which sexual issues are likely to be of concern to Margaret? What are the similarities between the two women?

The answers to all these questions have more to do with Josie and Margaret being women rather than one of them being disabled and the other able-bodied. This is because disability disadvantages women disproportionately to men in the following ways:

- disabled men are more likely to establish satisfying relationships than disabled women;
- disabled women are more likely to be divorced that disabled men;
- men's negative reactions are more extreme towards disability;
- disabled women are more likely to lack 'desirable' female qualities, such as physical grace and ease, so their body image is harder hit than that of disabled men;
- disabled married women with a non-disabled partner are subjects of curiosity, scrutiny and public misunderstanding (Asch and Fine, 1988).

It is commonplace to assume that knowing that one falls far short of socially ascribed standards of beauty or acceptability will result in negative self-image or poor self-esteem (Thomas, 1999), but all people, especially women, are hurt by the myth of perfection. Josie may have spent more time agonising over her bodily imperfections than Margaret and it would be patronising on her part to assume that she has more experience and/or understanding of the intricacies of sexual relationships. Swain et al (2003) challenge the tragedy model of disability on the grounds that not being able to make love in a straightforward manner means that a disabled person is compelled to experiment and therefore have a more interesting sex life than the average able-bodied person. They quote Paula, a disabled activist with MS:

> People say 'oh, you're a wheelchair user, this must mean you can't have sex', and I say 'why' and they say 'you can't walk' and I say 'oh, you walk while having sex?'. Two of the best lovers I had were wheelchair users. They were more imaginative. They were more sensitive and they were not performing. (pp 105-6)

Not feeling under pressure to 'perform' is also an advantage for disabled men. A man who is in a wheelchair after breaking his neck in a car accident comments on his sex life:

> One thing I know is that I'm a much better lover now than I ever was before. There are lots of reasons for that, but one of the biggest is that I'm more relaxed. I don't have a list of do's and don't's [sic], a timetable or a proper sequence of moves to follow, or a need to 'give' my partner an orgasm every time we make love. Sex isn't just orgasm for me; it's pleasuring, playing laughing, and sharing. (Lenz and Chaves, 1981, p 67)

Thus it is quite possible not only that Margaret knows a lot more about sex than Josie, but also that she has a healthier sense of self-esteem because, at 53, she will have developed an internally based body image or sense of body rather than something that is determined by the way society reacts (Bogle and Shaul, 1981). She may have specific problems relating to her recent wheelchair use; in particular, her opportunities to meet people may be more restricted. Knight (1981), herself a severely disabled person and sex therapist, says: 'If there is one single major problem in the area of sexuality and disability, it is the one killer called loneliness' (p 6).

Another possible similarity between Margaret and Josie is their sexuality. Either, or both of them, may be lesbian. Not only is it misinformed to view disabled people as asexual but neither are they necessarily heterosexual. Rousso's study of disabled women (1988) included lesbian or bisexual women, all of whom had also been involved in heterosexual activities in adolescence.

Although Josie may have studied disability on her training course and have expertise in particular impairments, it is Margaret who is the expert in how her condition affects her sexual activity. She will know what restrictions and limits govern her daily life and can be trusted to experiment sexually to find out what is possible. Thus, some useful questions Josie could ask are:

- In what ways has your disability made you a stronger person?
- What is good about your body?
- What needs to happen for you to lead a fuller life?

This section has included a large number of quotes from disabled people. This is done to give special emphasis to the service user voice, a voice that over the past 30 years has acknowledged difficulties but spoken against the tragedy model of disability. In the research for this chapter, the authors have been moved by the courage and expertise of disabled people and make no apology for ending with another piece of advice from a severely disabled person:

> I also think that our non-disabled brothers and sisters may not have the security of knowing that sexuality does not exist in the perfect body but in the pleasing body. We can help them overcome their handicaps. (Knight, 1981, p 9)

Talking to older people

The best predictor of longevity is a person's self-perception of well-being, so the promotion of good sexual health remains an important part of social work throughout the lifespan. Indeed, sexual activity is possibly even more important in older life in that it is an affirmation of the value of life (Terry, 1997). For couples, it maintains the pair bond and touching, caressing and shared delight assume a greater importance, with many older people saying that sex is 'better' than when they were younger. Not all older people have the opportunity to engage in sexual intercourse but, when they are asked about sexual activity, it is evident that older people are sexually active. Those who have been more sexually active decline more slowly and, where healthy, continue to have high enjoyment in sexual activity into their nineties (for an overview, see Read, 1999). As the older population has increased and the 'grey vote' becomes more influential, this is reflected in television programmes portraying sexual activity in older age in a more positive light than previously. What is not reflected in such programmes is that sexually active older people are at risk of sexually transmitted infections (STIs), the symptoms of which may be similar to other illnesses and may go unnoticed, especially as older people's sexual health is rarely screened (Squire, 2002).

Ageing of the reproductive system affects sexual *response*: both men and women's sexual arousal time lengthens, there are less contractions in orgasm, and the return to pre-arousal state is shorter than it is in younger people. This ageing process affects reproductivity but not proclivities (Medina, 1996). Thus sexual *interest* is not necessarily diminished, although stress, ill health, pain and disability could affect sexual interest. Healthy older people's interest in sex is more influenced by psychological and social factors.

Social factors adversely affecting sexual interest are largely to do with attitudes and opportunities, which may be reduced through lack of privacy and dependence. This is an area that has been increasingly recognised in residential care but there are many people in the community whose opportunities are restricted. For example, many older people suffer deterioration of their eyesight but remain perfectly healthy in other ways, yet there is evidence that their social care needs, particularly social contact, are largely unmet (Percival and Hanson, 2005). As with disabled people, loneliness can be a major issue. Older people may need to become more adventurous and experiment with different forms of sexual activity but they are the group least likely to be referred to psychosexual clinics, which are geared to the needs of younger and middle-aged people. Sex education for older people is rarely considered relevant to their needs.

Another factor adversely affecting sexual interest and activity is the attitudes of other people in older people's families. It can be very difficult for younger family members to see their ageing parents as sexually active people. This might be because they worry about their own inheritance when a parent looks like remarrying or it could simply be that the younger adult sees the parent only from their own perspective – how they fit into the younger family:

> Being disabled following a stroke means, apart from anything else, I'm more dependent on my children. My relationships with my lesbian friends have changed dramatically. My daughter is in a way relieved that she can think of me as a granny instead of as a lesbian, I'm respectable, I've even got a sort of status, but it means keeping quiet about the most important part of my life. I'm well looked after, but if I want to go to a gay pub or a

women's day concert, I have to arrange things with my friends, sneaking around like I did when I was a teenager. (cited in Young, 1999, p 154)

The main psychological factor inhibiting sexual activity in older people is the myth of the perfect body and the internalising of negative images of ageing bodies. The more positive portrayal of sexually active older people on television is not as explicit as it is with younger, more beautiful people and concerns about physical appearance can inhibit older people from considering themselves legitimate sexual partners. Although both older men and women tend to put on weight round the waist and lose elasticity in the skin, the ageing effects of the menopause mean that this occurs earlier in women. Because sex hormones affect tissue throughout a woman's body, loss of these hormones affect more than just the reproductive organs. Fat migration causes the most damage to a woman's body; fat migrates to the waist, causing sagging of the jaw and loss of elasticity to the neck, arms and thighs, and replaces mammary gland tissue, accelerating sagging of the breasts. Thus the loss of oestrogen greatly affects women's physical appearance and is not altogether prevented by hormone replacement therapy, which does not suit all women anyway. Disabled women are disproportionately affected, as they have a relatively higher rate of hysterectomy than non-disabled women as a means of managing menstruation and contraception (Bullock and McKenzie, 2003). Hysterectomy triggers early menopause, which has the capacity to make disabled women feel both aged and asexual, reducing their perceptions of their desirability as sexual partners. As research shows, women with learning disabilities are also disadvantaged in their struggle to make sense of the menopause because they have never fully, or even partially, understood the meaning and significance of menstruation (McCarthy and Millard, 2003).

Anthea is a 75-year-old woman who has lived on her own in assisted housing since the death of her husband three years ago. She asks your advice on how to access 'this botox that they have done on that programme where they make people look 10 years younger. I'd like my face done too'. She is afraid to ask her GP, since he ridiculed her request for hormone replacement therapy last year. She is still smarting at his comment that she did not need to think about that sort of thing at her age.

> What is your first thought about her request? Do you think she should be entitled to this sort of surgery on the NHS? Would your response be different if she had consulted you about the possible removal of unsightly warts on her face or about having contact lenses?

Although the ageing of the male reproductive organs is less pronounced and gradual, the notion of the perfect body increasingly affects men as well as women. For example, research shows that while gay men define for themselves the beginning of middle and old age roughly at the same time as heterosexual men, they define other gay men as beginning middle and old age some years earlier (Bennett and Thompson, 1991).

Grief is another psychological factor affecting sexual activity in older people. As discussed earlier, bereavement often results in diminished sexual interest. As bereavement in later life greatly increases the chances of early death but finding a new partner reverses this trend, the sexual well-being of older people is critical to their lifespan. Women and younger gay men are more likely to be bereaved because of the earlier death rate of men and the contribution of HIV (Ratigan, 1999). As noted earlier, younger family members may contribute to the lack of sexual interest experienced by older people by their expectations of celibacy on the part of the surviving parent, especially where they have enshrined the memory of the deceased parent. However, the picture for women is not all doom and gloom. Despite the dearth of older men and expectations that older women can cope with a loss of sexual activity, it is clear that many older women have found ways of being sexually active for many years. A common way is the use of sex toys but Brecher reported in 1984 that older women in his survey of 4,246 men and women aged 50-93 years solved the problem of the dearth of older men by taking a married man as a lover, while a small number 'made do' with a much older lover and a surprising number had a much younger lover.

Psychological factors also interact with social and physiological factors in a way that reduces sexual activity. For example, an elderly Asian lesbian who requires residential care runs the risk of being multiply marginalised as well as having her opportunities to meet a sexual partner reduced. Ethnicity and homosexuality raise particular problems for the social worker wondering how to address sexual issues; it cannot be presumed that gay men and women have benefited from human rights campaigns or that they are 'out', or that they are necessarily lacking cultural and community support.

The most important thing before talking to older people about sexual issues is for social workers to remain curious. They cannot assume anything, whether this be about sexual identity or sexual activity. All vary enormously. For example, it cannot be assumed that elderly same-sex couples are necessarily platonic friends or homosexual, or, if the latter, that they share the same meaning of what homosexuality means to them. Neither can it be assumed that sexual activity is more important to couples than to singletons, or that the former are more likely to be sexually active than the latter. A married couple may not have been particularly sexually active during their life and may welcome ageing as an 'excuse' to cease sexual activity altogether, while a single older person may be searching the internet for a partner. And some older people may wish to talk about sex but a lifetime of prudishness may prevent them from raising the issue.

> Both in their late seventies, Bill has been caring for Florence since she had a series of strokes and developed Parkinson's disease. He suffered a heart attack and the community care manager is of the opinion that Florence will be better cared for in a residential home. Bill is extremely upset at this idea, telling you, 'If she's with me I'm content. She's not an old boot to be thrown away. We've been married a long time. I miss her when she's not there'. He describes how they met and his eyes shine at the memory.
>
> *Regardless of the practical issues involved in making care arrangements for this couple, how would you talk to Bill about the meaning of his marital relationship? Does this couple's failing health alter their sense of intimacy?*

The dilemma is how to raise the subject without intruding inappropriately. Hughes (2000) suggests approaching the subject tangentially, that is, from common experience rather than special circumstances. Thus an opening might be: 'One of the things other people often find they really miss is the physical contact and touching'. Questions that relate to a person's sense of masculinity or femininity are also tangential ways of putting sex on the agenda. The use of 'hooks' described earlier is also helpful, as it allows the older person to signal an unwillingness to talk about sexual issues at the same time as it signals the social worker's willingness. As trust develops, the older person can then raise issues, if they are relevant. Should the older person not wish to talk about sexual issues, any assistance that promotes general physical health will be beneficial.

It was mentioned earlier that older people may need to find other ways to enjoy sexual activity because of pain from age-related conditions such as arthritis; this may take the form of experimenting with new ways of sexual intercourse or using sex toys. Despite the need for sex education in later life, this is rarely provided, yet there are many social care settings where it could be. Libraries could usefully stock sex manuals that show older and disabled people making love. An informative video of older men and women talking about their sex lives, their enjoyment of sexual pleasure, need for sexual fulfillment and ongoing exploration of their sexuality is *Living, Loving and Ageing* (Age Concern, 1989). Information on STIs can be found in *HIV and AIDs in Older People* (Age Concern, 1996).

Sexual well-being impacts on physical health, the quality of people's relationships and their identity; thus, it is an important component of overall health throughout the lifecycle. This is not always well recognised by social workers, as certain groups of people are storied as asexual (for example, older people whose sexual needs are rarely discussed), or as atypical (for example, lesbian and gay prospective adoptive parents whose sexual activities are often inappropriately discussed). Raising sexual subjects sensitively and appropriately is also difficult, as both social workers and their service users may be inhibited about discussing, or lack the language to describe, sexual issues. This chapter has suggested ways in which sexual issues can be introduced tangentially via the use of 'hooks' and the development of an appropriate language.

Further reading

Terry, P. (1997) *Counselling the Elderly and their Carers*, Basingstoke: Macmillan.

Summary

- The meaning of sexual activity shifts as adults begin to consider themselves as parents, becoming less explicit. There is a danger that social workers will focus on parenting issues and neglect associated sexual issues.
- The desire to have children is independent of sexual orientation but many lesbian and gay prospective adopters experience intrusive and inappropriate questioning about their sexual activities.
- Adults undergoing a child protection investigation and assessment have complex sexual needs that are often neglected.

- The effect of disability on sexual functioning is rarely given high priority by social workers, although most disabled people are either sexually active or aspire to be so.
- People who are disabled at an early point in their lives are the most likely to have received the least sex education, information and opportunities to talk about sexual concerns.
- Disabled women are less likely to establish satisfying sexual relationships than disabled men.
- When older people are physically healthy, they are as likely to be sexually active as younger people and their sexual activities as varied.
- Dependency and lack of privacy in older age pose particular problems for minority ethnic and/or gay and lesbian people.

Part Three
Sexual violence

This section looks at both those who commit and those who are subjected to sexual violence. The terms victim and offender are used, but with caution. They are labels that can subsume a range of behaviours, motivations, experiences and subjectivities into a 'shorthand' that can be unhelpful in addressing complexity.

Chapter Seven looks at working with victims of all forms of sexual violence, ranging from the intra-familial abuse of small children to the sexual exploitation of adults through international trafficking. Chapter Eight examines traditional approaches to working with offenders, outlining different programmes and detailing the research into their efficacy. Chapter Nine looks at newer practices with offenders.

SEVEN

Working with victims

Government guidance for social workers dealing with sexual violence is not as straightforward as that on sexual health. The latter emerged from a clear sequence of events: first, a concern was raised, in this instance the health risks resulting from teenage pregnancies and sexually transmitted infections; second, the people most at risk were identified; and finally a plan was put forward to prevent these risks, in this instance by improving the sexual health of all people. A similar process is evident with regard to sexual violence but, because sexual violence is so varied in terms of both victims and offenders, settings and effects, the guidance has emerged piecemeal. Historically, concerns were raised first about rape and then about child sexual abuse. Despite commonalities, especially the difficulties in establishing incidence because of under-reporting, these were researched discretely. As a result, the research literature is preoccupied with the effects of different types of abuse on victims. From this knowledge base, policies and practices were promoted in guidance from different government departments; for example, the Home Office published most of the early guidance on serious sexual assault and the Department of Health that on child sexual abuse, although the former issued guidance on offenders until it became clear that many sexual offenders were children themselves.

Making sense of the knowledge base on which government guidance developed was problematic for social workers. Estimates of incidence did little but demonstrate that sexual violence is widespread and under-reported – for example, recorded crime figures reflect only about 15% of all adult sexual violence (Home Office, 2005) – although the feminist emphasis in the early research tended to obscure the fact that sexual violence is also experienced by males. For example, the incidence of adult male sexual assault has been estimated at only 0.2% (Home Office, 2005), whereas other research indicates that 1% of adult males reported being sexually assaulted in 2003 (Sullivan, 2005). Similarly, the incidence of young males experiencing sexual abuse was underestimated in studies that extrapolated from adult female accounts of early sexual abuse but rose when institutional sexual abuse was studied. Neither are the research findings into the physical and mental health effects of sexual violence particularly helpful; practically every possible health effect has been noted, from irritable bowel syndrome and heart disease, to post-traumatic stress and borderline personality disorder, substance abuse and eating disorders (for an overview, see Itzin, 2005). Thus the therapies promoted in government guidance on a 'what works' basis are equally suspect as each therapy aims to treat the effects of 'different' forms of sexual violence, although there are some clear indicators about what sorts of therapies do not work for children.

What works for victims

What works for adult victims of sexual violence has not been as extensively researched as what works for child victims. Recommended victim care includes a wide range of counselling and emotional support via Sexual Assault Referral Centres where one-stop care is provided, Rape Crisis groups and more general Victim Support services (Home Office, 2005). Female prostitutes are especially at risk of sexual violence as well as being vulnerable to sexual health problems generally and report that they prefer services to be gender-specific and more easily accessible. They also benefit from specialised drug treatment programmes and sexual health services (Home Office, 2006b). Practical measures such as CCTV and legal taxis combined with awareness-raising publicity are also effective in reducing the risk of sexual assault by a stranger, although less effective in the instances of rape by a known person. Early interventions tended to be provided by women's support groups and were, therefore, predicated on feminist counselling approaches. More recently, cognitive behaviour therapy has been found to be effective. What works with victims of trafficking is less well understood but specialised care and protection, such as that offered by the Poppy Scheme (Home Office, 2006b), is recommended.

There have been many studies into the effectiveness of various therapies for child victims of sexual assault, which confirm the findings earlier summarised by Jones and Ramchandani (1999):

- although most children improve over time, a combination of time and therapy – of any sort – is more effective;
- all therapies are effective to some degree in improving anxiety-related symptoms, such as depressions and feelings of self-blame;
- offence-focused cognitive behavioural therapies are more effective with symptoms of aggression and behavioural disturbances;
- all therapies are most effective where they are embedded within good parental care and well-managed direct casework.

What does not work for victims

Many of the therapies for victims of child sexual abuse have been developed from professionals' experience of what worked with adult survivors of earlier abuse, despite the fact that their needs may be completely different. For example, adult survivors can find it difficult to break free from the abuse because they may still be in some kind of relationship with the abuser. This means that they are still living with self-blame and the responsibility for handling the abuse, as well as worrying about the safety of other vulnerable relatives. They may not have had the opportunity to talk about what happened or, if they have, they may not have been believed, and they may be plagued with flashbacks and/or difficulties in their adult sexual activity (for an overview, see Bass and Davis, 1988).

> Tania remembered her father's sexual abuse of her at the age of four after her partner, Robert, disclosed his previous sexual abuse after he was visited by the police as part of a larger investigation of sexual abuse in a boarding school. Tania is now plagued with terrifying flashbacks and is struggling to remember exactly what happened. The shape of various plants and sounds of some music remind her of incidental details of the abuse but she has no coherent memory, other than she feared for her life if she ever told what happened. Both Tania and Robert are receiving psychodynamic therapy, which they do not find helpful but are sticking with as it has been explained that their response to it is 'usual resistance'. They are unable to enjoy intimacy and cannot concentrate at work. In addition, Tania's father has just told her that his new, and much younger, partner is pregnant and he hopes that she will enjoy being an auntie. Tania has never told her mother about the abuse and Robert has never confided in his parents.
>
> *What are the legal, social, psychological and practical issues here? What would you consider to be the most urgent need? Do you consider that you are sufficiently well qualified and experienced to handle all aspects of the work? Should you refer an aspect of the work to a specialist, what would this be? How would you support any specialist work?*

Child victims are perhaps less likely to experience these difficulties as attempts will have been made to ensure their safety, provide them with opportunities to talk about their experiences, and make sense of what happened to them before they meet the challenges of adult sexual activity. The non-abusing parent will need support in a different way to that of the adult survivor, who may have been 'written off' because the survivor does not wish to upset them with news of something they may not have known about. Alternatively, in cases where the non-abusing parent of the adult survivor patently failed to protect, it may be that relationships have been long severed.

> Eight-year-old Nicola's long-term sexual abuse by a near neighbour and family friend came to light when her older cousin disclosed that he had abused her too. The case went to court but collapsed when Nicola was accused of making malicious allegations and she was unable to give coherent evidence. The abuser has returned to live opposite her home and she is unable to leave the home for fear of seeing him as he blows her kisses. The neighbours are divided in whom they believe. Her parents are supportive but the family in under intense stress due to a combination of financial difficulties following her father losing his job as a result of ill health and hostility from some neighbours.
>
> *What are the legal, social, psychological and practical issues here? What would you consider to be the most urgent need? Do you consider that you are sufficiently well qualified and experienced to handle all aspects of the work? Should you refer an aspect of the work to a specialist, what would this be? How would you support any specialist work?*

Research shows that adherence to therapies based on those that work for adult survivors are not only not always helpful but also sometimes downright harmful for children. Removing a familial abuser is not necessarily helpful, as it has the potential for making for difficulties in both the parent–child and parent–parent relationships as well as placing pressure on a non-abusing mother to protect in situations where she might be relatively powerless (Scourfield, 2003; Milner, 2004a). Child sexual abuse is rarely a sole problem; it coexists with family-based problems such as domestic violence, parental mental illness, substance abuse and parenting deprivation (whether or not it is intra- or inter-family abuse). Non-abusing parents are therefore extremely likely to have unmet needs of their own (Jones and Ramchandani, 1999). Corby's study of 40 child sexual abuse cases in three local authorities (1998) noted that while professionals understood the need to listen to children and take what they said seriously and sensitively, there was a tendency to focus on issues of sexual abuse at the expense of general deprivation, although they tended to be interlinked.

Doreen's children's names (Karen, aged 13, and Dale, aged 11) have been entered on the child protection register after it was discovered that her partner of 10 years is a Schedule One offender and has refused professionals access to his home. The case conference advised Doreen to eject him from the home but she is unable to do this as she is fearful of her safety – she has been a victim of his physical violence for many years; she has strong feelings of responsibility and affection for him as well as fears of failing in what is her second relationship; and she is dependent on him for financial support. On your first contact with her, she cries uncontrollably and tells you that she wants to safeguard her children's well-being but she does not want them all to lose the family home, which her partner is paying for. She is incapable of making a decision.

What are the main issues in this scenario? How best can you safeguard the well-being of both Doreen and the children?

Added to this, parents are expected to cope with their children's distress, and their own distress and guilt. Parents are typically shocked, frightened or withdrawn whereas the professional is not and may misjudge parental capacity to understand the allegations or protect their children.

Anita left her first husband after she discovered that he had sexually abused their two-year-old daughter, Louise. She has been happily remarried to John for 10 years and they have two children, Lily, aged seven, and Jonathan, aged four. She then discovered that John was taking pornographic photographs of Louise, who is now 16. She reported this to the police and social services immediately. John removed himself voluntarily from the home and began attendance on a sex offenders' course. He is permitted supervised contact with the children twice a week but they miss him very much and would like him to return home. Anita has undertaken a protectors' course but her final assessment reported that she used talk about the first abuse as a way of minimising the seriousness of the current situation and it is, therefore, considered that she is unable to protect the children. They recommended that she undertakes further work before contact with John is increased.

What do you consider to be Anita's main needs? Can these be met at the same time as the children's safety is ensured? How would you approach this task with Anita?

Removing children from home has been found to cause children more distress. This is partly because there are few specialist foster homes and partly because children who have been sexualised are vulnerable to further abuse because of the likelihood of being drawn into prostitution by association with other children in care homes (for an overview of the research into links between local authority care and entry into prostitution, see Cusik, 2002). It is also particularly problematic where the abuser is also a child of the family and where the abuse is complex; for instance, where the young abuser has been abused by older relatives and abuses his/her siblings in turn. As noted above, opportunities for widespread sexual abuse is common in families suffering from deprivation and/or dysfunction and, while one child's safety may best be ensured by the removal of another, victims experience sexual abuse differently depending on their relationship with the abuser. They often remain fond of the abusive child who has been removed and struggle to make sense of safety arrangements.

After Scott's parents split up, he lived with his mother and two older brothers. He was sexually abused by his elder brother, Adrian. His mother ejected Adrian from the home but as there were unsubstantiated allegations of sexually abusive behaviour by the other brother, Alan, Scott went to live with his father and new family. He has been happy with this arrangement, although he does not get on with his stepsister, Ellie, who is only one day younger than he is (15). He has been discovered in bed with his seven-year-old stepsister, Anna. When questioned, he confessed to abusing both Anna and his 10-year-old stepbrother, Dominic. He blamed Anna for getting into bed with him and inviting him to 'touch' her. Anna freely admitted that she had done this and it then emerged that Scott and Anna had been sexually abused by a family friend who used Scott's need to escape from the 'bother' Ellie created for him, and Anna's willingness to please, as a means to groom them. All the children have been diagnosed as having some degree of autism.

The family friend has been prosecuted and received a lengthy prison sentence. Scott has been returned to his mother's home under strict bail conditions. He has contact with his step-siblings at weekends, supervised by his father and stepmother, and is supervised at other times by his brother, Alan, who is still living with his mother. Scott wants to see much more of his step-siblings and they find it difficult to understand why he is not allowed to live with them. None of the children is showing any of the 'expected' effects of sexual abuse, other than Anna, whose sexualised behaviour at school is a cause for concern – she is making overtures to younger pupils at playtime.

How could you ensure the safety of all the children if Scott is allowed to have more contact with his father's family? What do you consider their main needs to be?

Failure to prosecute an abuser who is a family outsider is also associated with poor outcomes, as is encouraging the victim to go to court where there is an unrealistic chance of successful prosecution (Jones and Ramchandani, 1999). Adult victims are as badly affected as child victims by unsuccessful prosecutions; a three-year retrospective investigation into sexual abuse in a children's home resulted in only one (now elderly) care worker receiving a community sentence but 10 suicides among the victims identified, and a large number of adults in a high state of distress referred to the authors for counselling.

Philip's sexual and physical abuse in a residential special school for children with emotional and behavioural problems came to light after he was named as a victim by another resident. He has been interviewed by the police but refused to give evidence, as he has 'put all that behind him' and has built up a successful life with a 'lovely family'. He says that he is not coping well with work, having panic attacks, is unable to sleep, and is finding it difficult to relate to his six-year-old daughter, who is the same age he was when he was abused. No one has been prosecuted as a result of the police investigation and he tells you that he rues the day 'that policeman knocked on my door and brought it all back to me'.

Philip is the third adult who has been referred to you as a result of this investigation, all of whom are deeply distressed by the experience. What action would you consider taking? How best could you help Philip?

Keeping safe work when children are not told from whom they need to keep safe, or where they are provided with knowledge but not provided with opportunities to implement this knowledge in practice, is also an ineffective strategy (for an overview, see Mayes et al, 1992).

Jones and Ramchandani (1999) also noted that a significant number of children actually get worse after therapy – becoming more anxious, suffering more post-traumatic fears, becoming more aggressive and showing sexual behaviour problems. They suggest that therapy is likely to be harmful where the effects of harm are assumed, despite it being known that sexually abused children are not a homogeneous group: the assault may seem the same but it occurs over a range of psychosocial contexts and there is a variety of possible psychological outcomes, including being unaffected.

> Thirteen-year-old Sarah bunked off school to visit a local fairground, where she was orally raped by one of the fairground workers. The police have been unable to trace him, despite having solid forensic evidence. They are concerned that Sarah seems totally unaffected by her experience and have asked you to support her. She tells you that she knows what the man did was wrong and that she should not have bunked off school. She wants to return to school but cannot do so as the police have retained her school blouse and cardigan for forensic evidence and the key to her school locker containing her books is in the pocket of her cardigan. She is worried about being in trouble at school. She says her dad is 'no use. My mum died two years ago and he just sits about drinking and playing all the old records mum liked'.
>
> *What are Sarah's most urgent needs? How would you ensure her safety?*

Jones and Ramchandani (1999) also found that there was a group of children who described their therapy in negative terms, especially where they were required to talk about their abusive experiences. It is well established in the research that a victim of sexual violence needs to be able to make some sort of sense of the experience, particularly that they were not to blame, but not that they should necessarily be forced to talk about it:

> Although intense exploration of abuse is contra-indicated before stabilization is achieved, it is important to acknowledge the abuse at this stage ... counsellors should state that they consider the abuse to be a significant life experience but explain that it cannot be explored in greater depth until the client has certain resources and supports in place. (Draucker, 2000, p 36)

Bass and Davis (1988) make the point that not remembering the abuse has positive benefits for many victims:

- It can be more comforting for a child to deny reality than face the fact that the adults around her will not protect her.
- Forgetting, even as it happens, is the most common and effective way children deal with abuse.
- Fleeing the body through splitting comes naturally to children who may not have a memory at all.

They emphasise that there is no right or wrong when it comes to remembering but it seems to have become a mantra of some therapies that a victim must be able to talk in detail about the abuse before they can make sense of it and that the recovery is necessarily a long and painful process. Jones and Ramchandani (1999) also noted that avoidant coping styles are not as negative as some practitioners believe, although social workers have a tendency to direct children to long-term individual psychodynamic therapy despite short-term focused therapy not having usually been tried.

> As a result of severe emotional abuse and neglect, Nadia was removed from her mother's care and placed in the care of her maternal grandparents at the age of three. She became very aggressive and it was discovered that her grandfather had sexually abused her over a period of seven years. She has now been in long-term foster care for three years and her behaviour has improved; she no longer trashes her room or smears the walls with faeces, but she does exhibit a range of challenging behaviours. She has been receiving specialist psychodynamic counselling for 18 months to help her make sense of her abusive experiences. Her foster mother tells you that Nadia is very difficult to get to therapy and extremely disturbed for two days afterwards. She is also verbally abusive to the therapist. She has begged her foster mother not to take her, as she does not want to talk about what happened with her grandfather. As Nadia's caseworker, you have attempted to discuss this with her but she will not talk at all. You have consulted with the therapist, who tells you that Nadia's anger in session is a sign of progress as previously she would not talk at all, and that she needs to 'address the abuse as part of making sense of it'. The therapist is very experienced in this sort of work.
>
> *What are your responsibilities towards Nadia? What do you consider to be her most urgent needs?*

Therapies have not been very well developed for people who are most at risk of sexual violence, that is, women involved in what is euphemistically referred to as 'sex work'. While there is evidence that older male prostitutes and some women, notably those better educated, actively choose to offer sex for money and are able to keep themselves safe (Cusik and Martin, 2003), most women prostitutes run daily risks of sexual violence and emotional, physical and sexual ill health. A major contributory factor is addiction to Class A drugs, with many women engaging in sex for money while under the influence of drugs. Addiction also increases their dependence on pushers and pimps and means that their movements are controlled and that they have little choice in whom they accept as customers and little control over practising safe sex. Women working on the street are obviously vulnerable to sexual violence but off-street prostitution can also be very dangerous. The increase in migrant workers involved in off-street prostitution in major cities has increased to such an extent that the market has become saturated, driving down prices and increasing the incidence of unsafe practices (Dickson, 2004). Where these women are also victims of trafficking, the harm involved is considerable. Traffickers are known to have used rape/gang rape, abduction, torture and threats of violence against families to ensure the cooperation of their victims (Home Office, 2006b; Richards et al, 2006). What little research there is into this population of victims of sexual violence highlights a poor understanding of women's experiences (Refugee Women's Resource Project/Asylum Aid, 2005).

Myths about shared understandings

Although there is probably more agreement between professionals than was noted by Mayes et al (1992) about what constitutes child sexual abuse and whether to intervene, there are substantial differences about the definition of what constitutes adult sexual violence, particularly in cases of consent in rape where alcohol is involved. Debating different types of sexual violence to reach a consensus about possible causes and appropriate treatments creates narrow categories, emphasising differences and ignoring similarities. This leads to the persistence of myths about shared understandings, such as:

- The effects of sexual violence are the same for everyone, and necessarily damaging. *In fact, the effects are extremely varied.*
- Offenders are predominantly male and victims female. *In fact, males are as likely to be abused as females when they are in vulnerable situations, such as prisons and families.*
- We know what specialised therapy is needed and that it is suitable for all victims. *In fact, we do not know enough about the effectiveness of various therapies as victims' coping strategies vary enormously. We do know that therapies generally work best where they match people's preferred learning styles.*
- Prostitution is the 'oldest profession' and people choose to become involved in it. *Most women are trapped into prostitution in childhood, maintained in it through drug dependency, and suffer long-term damage as a result.*

- Sexual offenders are inherently recidivist. *The research evidence for this is addressed in detail later in this chapter.*
- One assessment is sufficient to estimate risk. *In fact, assessment needs to be fluid and ongoing as the needs of families change: 'This may be particularly important as the lexicon of risk assessment gains momentum, bringing false hope that through this process risk can be managed' (Jones and Ramchandani, 1999, p 48).*

Sexual violence has no clear boundaries; it can involve rape, sexual assault, child sexual abuse, trafficking, prostitution and internet porn, all of which have similarities in that they target vulnerable people. It is as likely to occur in families, prisons, schools, sports coaching, residential homes, friends' homes or on the street. Offenders can be fathers, mothers, family friends, lovers, babysitters, nursery workers, men in prison, teachers or older siblings. They can be homosexual or heterosexual. Thus a preoccupation with types and categories is not particularly helpful in working with a problem that is as much a social as an individual psychological problem.

Attempts at coordinating guidance

With growing concerns about links between domestic violence and sexual violence, adult and child prostitution, and trafficking, government has begun to coordinate responses:

- The Department of Health, National Institute of Mental Health and the Home Office are undertaking a mapping exercise of health and mental health service responses to victims of trafficking as part of a wider exercise looking at responses to victims of domestic violence and sexual violence, abuse and exploitation (Home Office, 2006a).
- The Home Office-coordinated strategy for developing routes out of prostitution will involve updating the guidance on safeguarding children involved in prostitution (Home Office, 2006b).
- The Common Assessment Framework now places child sexual health under the wider category of sexual health.

These initiatives have the potential to both clarify and broaden the role and duties of social workers in responding to sexual violence. Because of the links between family-based problems and vulnerability to both intra- and inter-family sexual violence, it is likely that social workers will be expected to play a significant role in preventing sexual violence occurring; take steps to ensure that people who have suffered sexual violence are safe in the future; and reduce the distress of both victims and their families.

The role of the social worker

Jones and Ramchandani (1999) hoped that their review of the research would support practice, not dictate it, with social workers examining it critically and taking out the messages that are helpful to practice. However, they also commented that studies of effectiveness in therapy tend to be randomised, controlled trials of the most specialised or detailed therapies and that these require lengthy and special training. As cognitive behaviour programmes lend themselves most easily to randomised evaluation studies, they are likely to have most prominence in the research literature, so do social workers all need to rush off to undertake specialised training, or refer service users to specialists? The authors of this volume would suggest not. Good outcomes are most likely to result from supportive parental care and well-managed direct casework, so social workers are pivotal to effective interventions, even where they involve specialist workers. At its most basic, it is a matter of putting sexual safety firmly on the agenda at an early stage of work with service users.

Preventing sexual violence

Preventative work can be effectively undertaken in all social care settings, whether this be family, group or community work, and all service user groups. As vulnerability to sexual violence is linked to family dysfunction, stress and deprivation, social workers can safely assume that most service users they see are vulnerable to some degree. For example, Doreen was trying to bring up two children at the same time as she was struggling financially and suffering from domestic violence; Nicola's family was plunged into debt following her father's illness; and Scott's family were coping with four disabled children. Although it is difficult to know whether the risk of becoming a victim of sexual violence has been reduced, any work that helps a family function better will have a protective effect for all its members. For example, if attention had been paid to Scott's difficult relationship with his stepsister, Ellie, he might have developed coping skills that did not require him to remove himself from the home and would not have been so vulnerable to sexual abuse. As he said: 'He [the abuser] knew that I needed to get out of the house for an hour or two and he played on that. I'm wiser now'. Similarly, Anna's disability rendered her vulnerable to exploitative adults and she would have benefited from keep safe work at an early stage.

Evaluation of keep safe programmes reveals serious limitations in their effectiveness; education changes what children say they would do in situations of sexual danger but they are not always able to do it when faced with a powerful and/or loved adult, and children with high self-esteem are more likely to use the information than children with low self-esteem (for an overview of the research, see Seal, 2004). Therefore the children most at risk – those already being sexually abused and with low self-esteem – were least well served by prevention programmes. Keep safe work with children who have been abused in the family needs to include keeping safe from the particular abuser. Where the abuser is involved in the keep safe work, they need to be prepared to refuse requests to touch the child's body. For example, a six-year-old girl went out to play in the paddling pool after a session on body privacy, returning to the room shortly afterwards and asking her father (who had abused her older sister) to help her put on her swimming costume. His willingness to pull it up around her waist but then telling her to pull the straps up herself 'because daddies don't touch girls on their boobie bits' (the words she used when colouring in the private parts of her body on a sheet of paper) reinforced the message of the session. Essex et al (1996) recommend that an agreed secret sign, such as a particular object being moved, or a stamped and addressed but blank postcard being provided, adds to safety where it is suspected that a child might be reluctant to tell a trusted adult. Anna's parents came up with the idea that she place a favourite toy in their bed if she had something she wanted to tell them but feared to do so.

Sexual abusers are not necessarily adult males; the authors' experience at Barnardo's The Junction service for children and young people whose behaviour is sexually concerning or harmful is that 'abusers' can be boys or girls, victims as well as offenders, and abusing peers or siblings. Even where a child or young person is removed from the home, there remain issues around the safety of other children in the residential home or school, or safety issues around contact. Social workers can, therefore, expect that sexual safety work with children will be a frequent part of their work.

Keep safe work with the children of asylum seekers involves sensitivity both to the special needs of children who may have been sexually, physically or emotionally traumatised in their countries of origin (Refugee Council/Department of Health, 2006) and to the cultural expectations of what can and cannot be included in sex education. Many refugee families are appalled by what they consider to be the lack of sexual morality of Western culture and will not give permission for their children to discuss keep safe strategies at school. Where they are willing, their children may not be settled in a school long enough to benefit from Personal, Social and Health Education. The authors have found that a specialised programme best fits this group of people's sexual safety needs; for example, Barnardo's The Junction in Rotherham is working with a multicultural agency to consult with mothers from many countries on how they wish the service to respond. As many refugee mothers may have been sexually traumatised themselves in their countries of origin, and may be living in male-dominated families, this is a way to help them tell their own stories.

In view of the known vulnerability of disabled children, especially those with multiple disabilities, ensuring that appropriate keep safe work has been undertaken is an essential part of *all* work with families with disabled children and adults with learning difficulties. Chapter Six discusses how this can be tailored to disabled children's specific learning styles but it is important to remember that a central issue is the amount of control a disabled child has over any event. Thus a discussion of good and bad touches and private parts needs to be undertaken sensitively with a child who has to be touched as part of their personal care. The authors have found that parents can come up with imaginative solutions when they are consulted on how best this can be done. For example, one mother of a severely autistic boy who was not fully potty-trained and had limited speech but was fluent in telephone numbers and obsessed with certain colours dressed him in the same coloured trainer pants to enable him to grasp the idea that only certain people were allowed to remove them. He was very vocal in protesting against any disruption of his routines and this was one way of utilising what could be difficult behaviour in other contexts. In other instances, children's physical and intellectual dependence results in them not having much of a voice, so care needs to be taken to ensure that adults or older siblings do not speak for them. For example, when keep safe work began with Scott and Anna, Scott was so anxious to give permission to Anna to say 'no' to him that he was in danger of bullying her into submission and this had to be pointed out to him. Where children have no speech at all, Talking Mats are one way of communicating (see Chapter Six for details). For vulnerable adults with no speech, Iveson (1990) adapted the family therapy technique of including an absent person as a means of including a non-speaking person. In the extract below, Saleha is a 23-year-old woman who is paralysed from the neck down. As she cannot speak, no one knows for certain what she understands, although most people think she can understand something:

Iveson: Mrs Bibi, if Saleha *could* speak and I were to ask her to choose someone to speak for her at this meeting, who do you think she would choose?

Mrs Bibi: (After long thought) I think she would choose Muni (the younger daughter).

Iveson: Do you also think she would choose you, Muni, or do you think she would choose someone else?

Muni: I would have said she would choose mother.

Mrs Bibi: No, you and she have an understanding …

Mani: (The eldest daughter) I think she would choose Muni, too. They've always been close even though they do argue.

Iveson: So, Muni, will you agree to be Saleha's 'voice' for this meeting?

Muni: Yes.

Iveson: Well, what I'd like you to do is when I want to ask Saleha a question, I want you to answer it as if you were Saleha. Will you be able to do that?

Muni: But I might not get it right.

Iveson: No, I'm sure you won't get it right all the time because you're a different person but I'd still like you to do it. Will you?

Muni: Yes.

Iveson: It will mean that sometimes you'll have to speak twice, once for Saleha and once for yourself. (Everyone laughs.) Saleha, your sister is going to speak for you but because she is not you, she might not get it right. If she does get it right, would you lean your head towards her and, if not, lean your head towards your mother (she was sitting between the two), and I'll ask her to try speaking for you. (Iveson, 1990, pp 81-3)

The authors of this volume have adapted this technique for children who are too embarrassed to answer questions. A parent is interviewed as the child, who is given two cards, one with RIGHT and one with WRONG written on it. The child holds up the appropriate card after each answer. As the questions become more detailed, the parent-as-child is unable to answer them and usually says 'You speak, I don't know', or the interviewer will say 'I think [name of child but pointing to parent] is having some difficulty. Can you help her out?'. As the child has enjoyed correcting a parent, they often take over the answering at this point.

Where one or both parents' capacity to protect is impaired because of mental illness, substance abuse or domestic violence, for example, keep safe work can usefully include a wide area of safety issues. In the authors' experience, following the discovery of intra-familial sexual abuse involving children, where the social worker is asked to assess the risk the offending child poses and undertake keep safe work with the victims, there is often a concerned mother but one whose capacity to protect is limited by her drinking. Children not only become depressed over maternal drinking, but are also unsupervised in a variety of situations. For example, one adolescent offender had extra responsibilities placed on him during his mother's drinking binges and his younger sister was left to roam the streets. As well as the risk to her sexual well-being posed by her brother, she was vulnerable to becoming the victim of a road accident, assault by a stranger, bullying by peers and burns (she was smoking and playing with candles both at home and at her friend's house). Thus her keep safe plan involved all these issues. 'Keeping safe when mum drinks' also became an item when it became clear that her mother had only limited control over her drinking. This necessitated adding adults outside the home to her Helping Hand (see Chapter Four), ensuring that their telephone numbers were in her mobile phone directory, that she could remember where she had put her mobile phone, that she had sufficient top-up credit on her mobile, and that the adults named on her Helping Hand were aware of the need to respond quickly to any requests from her.

Fourteen-year-old Martin has a long history of sexual activity. He was abused at age seven by a family friend; he was found in bed with a slightly younger boy at 12; he touched a vulnerable girl at school inappropriately at age 13; and there are suspicions that he has 'touched' his six-year-old sister, Maisie. His mother has a long history of taking overdoses and she has been diagnosed as depressed and as having a borderline personality disorder. She copes with 'down days' by taking tranquillisers and sleeping through them. This can take two days. Other days she is lively and makes demands that Martin show her more respect. Maisie is in foster care, with supervised contact at the home, but the whole family hopes to be reunited shortly. They also hope to be rehoused as they have experienced hostility from neighbours.

How would you ensure Maisie's safety? What do you consider Martin and his mother's needs to be? How would you meet these?

Where social workers are involved in group work, this is usually because a particular concern has been identified, and this will form the focus of the work. Whether the aim of the group work is to prevent youth offending, promote good mental health in adults or provide support to parents with disabled children, there is scope to discuss vulnerability to sexual violence. Merrill's (1999) outline of how to run a sexual violence prevention group for lesbian, gay, bisexual and transgendered young people is a useful resource here. As well as the sexual safety issues discussed earlier, this is an appropriate forum to discuss mobile phone and internet porn. Young people's access to porn is widespread and not always consciously sought; for example, any person with a Bluetooth wireless technology device can send a pornographic message to anyone else in the same room with the same facility. The simple solution for parents is to ensure that their children have limited facilities on their mobile phones. Accessing porn via the internet or email is incredibly easy. During the research for this book, the authors typed 'government guidance and sexual exploitation' into a Google search on the internet and found themselves in a site advertising hard core porn. The only check was the warning: 'If you are under eighteen years old or likely to be offended, please click the "back" link now'. As a curious teenager is unlikely to do this, parents need to protect them by subscribing to a service such as Net Nanny, Cyber Patrol or Surf Watch. Checking whom children are talking to on the internet is also part of sexual safety. Raising these issues in group work provides parents with the opportunity to benefit from other parents' research into internet safety, and children and young people with an opportunity to discuss the effects of porn on attitudes towards women and children.

Social workers who work in group settings such as residential units may not be involved in planned group work around a specific issue but they are well placed to prevent sexual violence. Children's homes have potential for increasing the risk of sexual violence because they are especially likely to have residents who have been removed from home because they are victims or perpetrators of sexual violence, or both. It is well established that young people often enter prostitution as a result of associating with young people already in prostitution. It is also becoming clear that young people risk sexual assault in children's homes and generally do not report it. Where they do, it tends to be minimised by staff, particularly when it involves a young woman with a history of 'promiscuity' (Barter et al, 2004). At the very least, residential social care workers can usefully devise sexual safety rules in conjunction with their residents and ensure that a safe care plan is on display in the home (see Figure 7.1).

Figure 7.1: Safe care/keep safe plan

SAFE CARE/KEEP SAFE PLAN

Bedroom and bathroom doors to be shut if you are getting dressed or washed	
If you are on the toilet or in the bath, remember to shut the door	
PJs/nightie and dressing gown to be worn when you are downstairs	
Do not go downstairs without clothes on	
If you want to talk to someone and they are in their bedroom, knock on the door first – don't walk straight in	
Everyone should get dressed in their bedroom or bathroom	
No play fighting	
We all have someone to talk to if we are not feeling safe	
Everyone to be in by their agreed 'in times'	

Similarly, residential social care settings providing both long-term and respite care for disabled children and adults can inadvertently increase vulnerability to sexual assault. General safety issues are likely to be addressed as part of independence training, such as mobility and cookery programmes, but sexual safety is often neglected. This is especially likely when a resident only stays for one or two days' respite care each month. Again, a safe care plan can be drawn up to protect residents; see, for example, the plan drawn up for Callum, below. Callum is 16 but functions at a seven-year-old level and tends to prefer playing with much younger children as he is bullied by older children. He has recently begun to touch young children inappropriately when playing out at home. His respite care home has a number of young, vulnerable residents, one of whom (Anthony) seeks physical contact indiscriminately.

Figure 7.2: Callum's safe care plan

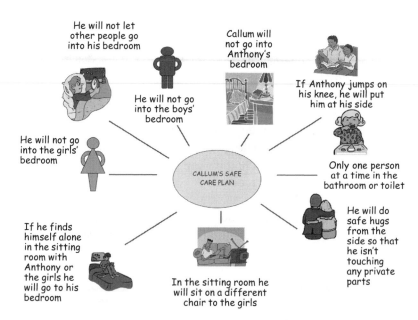

He will not let other people go into his bedroom

Callum will not go into Anthony's bedroom

If Anthony jumps on his knee, he will put him at his side

He will not go into the boys' bedroom

He will not go into the girls' bedroom

CALLUM'S SAFE CARE PLAN

Only one person at a time in the bathroom or toilet

He will do safe hugs from the side so that he isn't touching any private parts

If he finds himself alone in the sitting room with Anthony or the girls he will go to his bedroom

In the sitting room he will sit on a different chair to the girls

Few social workers are involved in community work in the sense that a specific community is the focus of their work, but they do work alongside community workers such as housing support workers, community psychiatric nurses, outreach addiction workers and women's aid support workers. Marshalling these sources of support is much more effective in preventing sexual violence if attention is paid to where vulnerable service users are housed. Plans to integrate service users into the community are often limited by the need to accept housing that is readily available. This is most likely to be in an area where people less vulnerable do not want to live and is, therefore, an area where vulnerability to sexual assault is high. Research into teenage prostitution associated with drug use (Milner et al, 2002) revealed care leavers and young single mothers being housed in an area of significant deprivation:

- Sixty-five per cent of the population was in Council Tax Band A, and a further 14% in Band B.
- The population was unbalanced with a preponderance of young and old people, and people from ethnic minorities.
- The overall mortality rate was 15% higher than average, and there were more road casualties.
- A local crime audit showed that crime was seriously under-reported.
- There were a high number of drug users and asylum seekers in the area.
- There were no female doctors and the local GP practice had closed its list to drug users.
- Both the local health centre and the junior school were protected by high railings with metal spikes.
- Professionals were afraid to work in the area because of the overt presence of pimps and drug pushers, many of whom were armed.
- There was evidence of both young women and young men being involved in off-street prostitution.

If vulnerable young people and adults are to be safeguarded against sexual assault and exploitation, they require safe housing. Social workers can raise this at multi-agency meetings and refuse to move people into areas where they themselves are afraid to work. Similarly, care needs to be taken over the allocation of flats to young homeless people in special housing association properties. Despite the provision of support workers attached to many of these schemes, in the course of their practice the authors met with many young people who complained that drug-using neighbours burst into their flats unannounced and that they are harassed on the streets. Housing vulnerable young people in close proximity acts as a magnet for pimps and pushers, as do many children's homes. Where young people are being groomed by pimps and are afraid to give evidence against them, social care workers have found abduction law to be more effective than child protection legislation.

> Eden has lived in a one-bedroomed council flat in an area notorious for drug dealing and gang violence since her mother threw her out. She has been raped by a known man and now feels frightened, sick and ashamed. She says that she has coped with things like this before but now she feels that it is her fault for being gullible and naïve. She had welcomed this man as he was very protective of her and she felt safe going out with him. She dare not go out in case she meets him or members of his family. She gave up her job six months ago after her cousin was made redundant and could no longer give her a lift to work in his car. She does not want to live in a refuge as she lived briefly in a hostel for homeless young women and was beaten up by one of the residents.
>
> *What are Eden's main needs? What action would you take to ensure her safety?*

Ensuring safety

On the face of it, removing the abuser is the simplest and seemingly most effective way of ensuring safety, whether by ejecting an intra-familial abuser from the home; serving a banning order; imposing strict bail conditions and hoping for a conviction and lengthy prison sentence; or rehousing a vulnerable victim, such as Eden. Obviously, offenders should take responsibility for their actions and be punished but this should not be confused with safety. Removing the offender from contact with the known victim is only a partial solution. In the first place, it might not be what the victim and family want. Where the abuse is intra-familial, both the victim and family may not wish the relationship to be severed, although they will want the abuse to stop. It might be that one member wants the offender removed but other family members do not. This creates problems for a victim who is conscious that they are responsible for breaking up the family. For example, a teenage victim may wish to be safe from an abusive father but recognise that younger siblings want him to stay. Contact with children can also be used as a means of harassing a partner, as can an offender's insistence on being present at child protection case conferences.

In the second place, removing the offender is only a temporary solution, as offenders are released from prison eventually, leaving victims with the fear of retaliation at a later date. Offenders are also likely to return to the area where they and the victim live as they often have relatives there. These relatives and their friends may well disbelieve the victim or blame them for getting the offender into trouble. Thus the victim can face hostility from neighbours as well as feel unsafe in their home area. Where there are restrictions on the offender approaching the victim, these do not protect the victim from seeing the offender in the locality and worrying about bumping into them accidentally. In one case handled by the authors, a young woman met the man who had knocked her off her bike in a park and raped her a year previously in a record shop. He approached her and said: 'I see you're spending the compensation money you got out of me'.

> Fourteen-year-old Olivia has been raped by a pupil from her school after he followed her into a toilet at a party. He has been excluded from the school but continues to live with his family only three streets away. He is popular with other pupils in his year and the boys are aggressively hostile to Olivia, taunting her in the playground by lifting up her skirt and shouting, 'Rape! Been there, done that'. The girls are ignoring her. Olivia is refusing to go to school but her parents are insisting that she return to sit her exams.
>
> *How best can you ensure Olivia's safety?*

In the third place, while removing the offender provides some protection for the known victim/s in the short term, unknown victims remain at risk. For example, placing a young offender in a children's home with other vulnerable young people still requires safety planning. Where an offender is sent to prison, there is little protection for vulnerable prisoners, other than the use of segregation. Where a partner wishes to retain a relationship with an offender, removing the children does not reduce risk either; as one mother said when she lost her baby to adoption as a result of her partner's Schedule One status: 'It's like saving only one baby from a burning building. What about all the other babies?'. There are also situations where sexual abuse is suspected but strongly denied, and it is difficult to ensure safety in these instances.

The reality is that life is not very safe for many people and they need a range of safety strategies if they are to regain trust and a sense of freedom. In the early stages of managing intra-familial child sexual abuse, a 'quick safety fix' is useful, such as the establishment of a set of safe care rules for a family. While this ensures safety in the short term, the plan will need to be reassessed and revised to prevent 'slippage'; for example, the protector who is monitoring the plan cannot guarantee not to be ill; parents may well not trust babysitters but they do need to be able to go out together occasionally; and family circumstances change. The burden of monitoring a safety plan often falls on mothers, which is unfair; and, as we have seen, sexual violence coexists with family problems so a mother or father may not be able to maintain the vigilance of early responses. Where the offender continues to live with the family, or where abuse is denied, safety plans need to be developed so that the offender takes responsibility for monitoring their own behaviour and the victims have a means of alerting other people quickly.

Fifteen-year-old Jack has been living in a children's home since he was charged with the rape of a nine-year-old girl who was a friend of his sister. Previously, he lived with his mother, sister and 10-year-old brother. He is supervised at all times in the children's home; he is not attending school as he fears being beaten up by his victim's older brother; and he is supervised on twice-weekly contact with his family. He is deeply ashamed of his offence but is unable to talk about it, other than to say he will never do it again. He wishes to return home and his family wants him back.

What would an adequate safety plan look like before you could consider Jack going home? What could Jack tell you that would convince you that he is safe around young children?

For adult victims of sexual violence, safety planning needs to address vulnerability in a wide range of situations. Many victims say that they avoid going out without an escort, wear 'big clothes' or increase their attempts at appeasement. All these behaviours mark the person out as a potential victim; as one young woman remarked after a third rape: 'What's the matter with me? Does it say "rape me" on my forehead?'. In one sense, she might as well have had the words written on her forehead, as she unconsciously signalled this by her demeanour; she walked around with her head down, she was timid in contact with people, and she burst into tears easily. All these things were completely understandable in the light of her traumatising experiences but they emphasised her vulnerability. To assist her develop safety strategies that would work for her, it was important to get her to identify what control she had over her life and what would be reasonable safety responsibility taking. One way of achieving this is to identify the strengths a person has developed as a result of the abuse; for example, Bass and Davis (1988) ask victims of abuse: 'Think what it's taken for you to survive. What are the qualities that enabled you to make it? Perseverance? Flexibility? Self-sufficiency? Write your strengths with pride' (p 39). The victim can then decide how to keep safe in a range of potentially dangerous situations, such as not getting drunk; holding a bottle while dancing to avoid it being tampered with; going to the toilet in pairs; pre-booking a taxi from a known firm; sitting at the front of a bus, near the driver or near older adults; and having car and house keys to hand. These involve reasonable personal responsibility taking and are within a person's control.

Where adults are sexually assaulted by a partner (reported inter-spousal sexual violence is mainly heterosexual male-on-female violence but there are instances of gay and lesbian people who have experienced sexual violence within intimate relationships), ensuring safety can be complex. As with domestic violence more generally, it is difficult for a man or woman to leave a loved one, not least because it involves admitting that the relationship has failed. Moreover, there are practical and financial considerations that prevent a person leaving a sexually abusive partner; these may be interpersonal, such as the difficulty in disentangling a joint mortgage, or community-based, such as the lack of appropriate refuge provision for gay and lesbian people. As such victims already have experience of powerlessness, it is especially important that these complicating factors are taken into consideration when devising safety plans. Exhorting a person to remove themselves from the abusive situation merely adds pressure to an already distressed person, and lengthy support may be needed before an entirely satisfactory safety plan is devised.

Asma married against her parents' wishes, and her own doubts, but she believed that her partner would change once he learned to trust in her love for him. In the early stages of their relationship, he was physically abusive and this has escalated since the birth of their baby son 18 months ago. He knocks her to the ground and sits on her chest, pulling her hair, saying that he will not let her get up until she has stopped crying. When she stops crying, he forces her to have sex – she agrees to this because she knows the violence will then stop for a week or so – and then he tells her that he loves her and that she enjoys sex with him. The sexual violence is the part of his abusive behaviour that she loathes most. She is desperate to leave him but has not been able to do this yet as he is a good father to their son, and he looks after him while she works and studies part time; he owns their house; and he has threatened to follow her anywhere she goes. Her parents are supportive and would take her back but she does not want to live with them and 'be a child again'. She did live in a refuge for a short while but was very unhappy there.

Ensuring the safety of women in prostitution is more complex; the abuser/s cannot easily be removed, whether they are pimps and pushers or punters. The Ugly Mugs scheme that alerts women to known dangerous customers is one way of safeguarding women (Home Office, 2006b) and government is considering changing the definition of a brothel. Currently, two or more women working together or one with a maid constitutes a brothel and encourages women to work in isolation. Government is also committed to reducing drug dens as means of increasing safety. Prostitutes report that outreach is indispensable; for example, the Nottingham Prostitute Outreach Workers Project (POW) reported that most of the women using the service did so 'as a "one stop shop" and did not use any other health or social service providers' (Gillies et al, 2004, p 5). The range of services provided by POW includes:

- advice on sexual and general health, personal safety, drug use, lifestyle changes, exiting from prostitution, family planning and provision of services by other agencies;
- information delivered by word of mouth; leaflets developed by clients on sexual health, drugs, possibilities in education, language cards and 'dodgy punter' information; and leaflets from other service providers;
- free condoms distributed during outreach and drop-in sessions;
- practical support in matters relating to homelessness, safe practices, exiting, health appointments, court appearances, welfare rights, safe accommodation, domestic violence, routes to education and training, and crisis intervention;
- basic counselling around lifestyle choices;
- emotional support concerning domestic violence, partner drug use, health worries and hospital visits;
- referrals to other agencies and chaperone services;
- advocacy through the organisation of workshops and presentations at conferences;
- a pen-pal service for clients in prison, drug rehabilitation units, hospital and those who have exited prostitution;
- access to a clothes bank (POW, 2004).

Engaging women with services that can help them take the first step to finding a route out of prostitution is difficult as it involves a complete lifestyle change. Gillies et al (2004) found that where an outreach service develops networks and supports prostitutes – and their families and friends in the neighbourhoods in which they live – clients trust the organisation and say how important this is in helping them make necessary changes in their lives. To make these changes, work here needs to address addiction; unstable housing; health needs; skills training in managing a tenancy, claiming benefits and accessing education and employment; and counselling for mental health problems associated with experiences of violence (Home Office, 2006b).

The safety needs of women who are trafficked are more complex as they face threats in all aspects of their lives. For example, the police may be pressing them to give evidence against traffickers who are threatening their families. They are also likely to be in the country illegally and under threat of deportation, where there are further dangers. There is evidence that the Home Office calls for their protection on one hand (Home Office, 2006b) but makes this difficult by refusing their claims for asylum on the other (Richards et al, 2006). This latter study establishes the needs of this group as an extension of the needs of all asylum-seeking and refugee women in that they need help with applications to the Home Office, physical safety, practical support, time to prepare their cases, and time to come to terms with the reality of their situation and levels of trauma experienced. Support programmes for trafficked women need, therefore, safe housing, sensitive translation services and long-term, patient follow-up.

Reducing stress for victims and their families

As has been noted, there is a tendency for social workers to focus on the offence and its emotional effects, rather than the possible variety and range of problems associated with it. Poorly handled initial contact is associated with poor emotional outcomes (Jones and Ramchandani, 1999), so it is important that distress is reduced by well-managed casework that supports both victims and their families. A first consideration is how to support these people through possible legal processes. Although failure to prosecute a family outsider is associated with poor outcomes, the first step is to assess how realistic the chance is of getting a conviction. Giving evidence in court is a distressing situation where a person's integrity will be questioned, and they will have to relive the violence. In addition, delays in getting cases to court prevent people from getting on with their lives. To devote a lengthy period of one's life to preparing for court and enduring being cross-examined is only reasonable where the victim strongly wishes to proceed and there is a realistic chance of conviction. This is especially the case with victims who have learning difficulties. Crimes against people with learning difficulties are frequent but under-reported (Sharpe, 2001) and, where they are reported, victims are often not considered reliable witnesses because of possibly defective memories, susceptibility to suggestion and a lack of accurate reporting skills (Cooke and Davies, 2001). Government guidelines recommend that social care workers ensure that they take special care in their initial interviews by:

- slowing down their speech rate;
- allowing extra time for witnesses to take in what has just been said;
- providing time for the witness to prepare a response;
- being patient if the witness answers slowly;
- avoiding immediately posing the next question;
- avoiding interrupting.

Questions should:

- be easily understood;
- not contain jargon or abstract ideas;
- make only one point;
- not be too directive or suggestive;
- not contain double negatives.

Special measures are also available to assist the witness in court, such as screens, removal of wigs and gowns, video evidence and the use of a cognitive interpreter as intermediary. An empowerment scheme in South Africa (Dickman and Roux, 2005) resulted in a conviction rate for people comparable with the best conviction rate in the general population. This scheme evaluated witness levels of intellectual functioning and understanding of sexuality, and ability to consent to sexual activity, and then provided comprehensive support before and during court cases for both victims and families.

Having ensured safety and decided whether it is reasonable to prepare the victim for court proceedings, the next task of the social worker is to support the family or carers. This may seem the wrong way round but a supportive family will be more able to protect in the future and more able to offer long-term, consistent support for the victim, thus reducing the need to provide specialist emotional support. This involves recognising parents' and carers' needs, and responding to them. They are likely to be shocked and dismayed, possibly overcome with guilt, and they may have to make difficult decisions about who can and cannot be in their home. This is particularly true where the abuse involves sibling groups, as this list of comments from a parents' group shows:

- 'I thought, "I'm going to have to move. Everyone's going to know".'
- 'I was beside myself. I couldn't sleep, couldn't think about anything else, couldn't even tidy up a room.'
- 'Where does it come from, this behaviour? I thought I brought them up well enough for them to know right from wrong.'
- 'How to support one and keep the other one safe? You can't turn against one, you need to find that balance' (Barnardo's, 2005).

Another group of parents likely to be very distressed and torn between what actions to take are black mothers. Bernard's (2001) study of black mothers' experiences of child abuse investigations found that the complex power relations in black families mean that black mothers are often caught between their own needs and wishes, and the expectation of families and partners that they be loyal. This further complicated the way professionals view black men in families. Where mothers have divided loyalties, it does not help to accuse them of putting their needs before those of their children; these are very real relationship complications that require sensitive support and understanding. In supporting families and ensuring safety, it is important to avoid adding to their sense of guilt and self-blame; they will probably already be blaming themselves enough for their parental shortcomings. Freeman et al (1997) found that externalising parental guilt is helpful – separating the problem (guilt) from the person by talking about it as something that moved in with the family, and how it is supported by social expectations of what constitutes good parenting. This frees parents up to remember that they have strengths and abilities. Some useful questions for parents in this situation include:

- How have you dealt with problems successfully in the past?
- When have you worked really well as a family in the past to sort things out?
- How have you managed to keep your child safe in the past?
- What works best for you as a parent?

- What would you say is the best thing about your family?
- What is your biggest success as a family?

The partners of adult victims of sexual violence also need support in much the same way as parents. An extra difficulty that partners may have is a doubt about the lack of consent. This is partly to do with myths about rape, especially where the offender is known to the victim, and the tendency on the part of the accused to plead that it was consensual. Gay victims of rape are particularly vulnerable to being misunderstood, as gay culture often holds that men are supposed to want and enjoy sex pretty much whenever it is available, 'so if sex is forced, is it rape, or is it just bad sex?' (Allen and Leventhal, 1999, p 80). Letellier (1999) describes being raped by his partner as a follow-up to physical violence, his slow coming to terms with what happened to him, and the reactions of subsequent partners:

> As the years tick by, I test the waters and occasionally tell a sexual partner that sex can be difficult for me because I was … raped. They almost always furrow their eyebrows. Gay men don't use that word when they talk about themselves. I do. (p 10)

Reducing distress for victims

This chapter uses two words usually avoided by the authors – victim and offender. These words are generally avoided because they are not satisfactory in explaining fully the complexities of sexual violence, not least being that many people often occupy both roles at the same time. The choice of words here is deliberate to make the point that a person who experiences sexual violence is, quite simply, a victim of crime. In many respects, it would be simpler to abandon the terms child abuse, rape and domestic abuse. Instead, we could use the terms that describe other assaults – occasioning actual bodily harm, grievous bodily harm and so on. This would then facilitate supportive efforts that are individualised, rather than focusing on different categories of sexual violence. Dolan (1998) makes the point that many therapies talk about the need for a 'victim' to move to 'survivor' as part of the healing process but that this can limit people's futures, as life is constantly filtered through the window of survivorhood. She suggests that this diminishes people's capacities to fully experience and enjoy life, contributing to the flatness and low-grade depression reported by so many self-described 'survivors'. The task of the social worker is to facilitate a person's full return to a satisfying life where their highest hopes and aspirations are regained. Thus the first question would be: 'What are your best hopes for yourself?', followed by 'Where would be best for you to start on fulfilling these hopes?' or 'Where is the easiest place to start?'. This may well not be to talk about the abusive experience in depth and a reluctance to talk about this should be respected: 'It is imperative that the client does not feel intruded upon, lest the invasive aspects of the original trauma be symbolically re-enacted' (Dolan, 1991, p 165). Where a person does talk about what happened to them, it is important to accept their definition of the assault; for example, a lesbian woman may describe what happened to her as rape, even though it would not fit the legal criteria. The appropriate emotional, practical and social support needed will emerge from a person's answers to these questions. The following section presents ideas about how some of the common problems associated with sexual violence can be worked with in helpful and respectful ways.

Offenders claiming that adult sexual violence was consensual or telling a child that the child made them do it, means that their victims often take an unreasonable amount of responsibility for what has happened. Children who self-blame can be helped to realise the power imbalance underpinning their vulnerability by asking them to draw stick figures of themselves and the person who initiated the sexual behaviour. They are then asked who is the biggest, how bigger/older people should care for little kids and so on. This can then be followed up

Figure 7.3: Good touches/bad touches

WHEN TOUCHING PRIVATE PLACES IS GOOD AND OK,
AND WHEN IT IS WRONG AND MAKES PEOPLE UNHAPPY

YES	NO	NO	NO
Between two adults who love and care about each other and have the same amount of power	Not between an adult and a child because the adult has all the power and the child doesn't understand	Not between a big kid and a little kid because the big kid has all the power	Not between kids because it is too confusing

Source: The Junction, 10 Nightingale Court, Moorgate, Rotherham S60 2AB.

by using a chart that explains who can touch and who cannot, as shown in Figure 7.3.

Small children need explanation and reassurance about power differentials but this is not likely to be helpful with older people who have internalised societal expectations for managing sexuality, such as 'not asking for it' or 'surely he could have fought back'. These ideas are likely to be stronger where the assailant was a known person and the victim takes unreasonable responsibility for allowing it to happen or not seeing it coming. Self-blame is better undermined than tackled head on by asking questions such as 'What will you be doing/thinking differently when you no longer blame yourself for what happened?' or by asking the person to make a list of what is reasonable safety taking. Where a person is stuck in self-blame, asking them to write therapeutic letters can be helpful:

• Write a letter to the person who did these things to you, saying how it affected you, including the impact of their words and actions. Also, state what sort of response you expect from that person. This letter is not for posting. Take as much time as you need over this letter but stop writing it if you become distressed.
• Write an imaginary response from the person who wronged you, including all the excuses they would make about their actions and how they would lay the blame on you.
• Write a different response from that person; one that fully acknowledges the impact of their actions on you and offers a satisfactory apology (adapted from Dolan, 1998, pp 145-6).

The first letter enables the person to articulate and acknowledge what happened to them and, as these may be feelings that the person does not wish to talk about with you, it is important that you do not ask to read the letter unless the person offers to share it. It is common to find that the letter has been destroyed before the next session as it has served its purpose.

The second letter helps the person to understand that they were not to blame as they see the list of pathetic excuses in print – and have the opportunity to reread them. The third letter allows them to acknowledge that they deserve a full apology. Even though they are unlikely to get it, it helps them to forgive themselves. Both these letters are commonly shared at later sessions.

Encouraging people to value themselves is also helpful in undermining self-blame, increasing self-esteem and reducing flashbacks and intrusive thoughts. This can include asking a person to make a list of good things about themselves; identify their strengths; and pamper themselves with small treats (for a fuller discussion, see Milner, 2001).

Disassociation of the body is a common way in which people, especially children, protect themselves from the full horror of sexual assault. This can affect sexuality in a number of ways: a child may become overly sexualised, a young person may indulge in reckless sexual activity, and an adult may find sexual relations with a partner problematic. All of these behaviours can be helped by encouraging the person to value themselves, and being willing to listen and talk about what the person will be doing when they are able to feel comfortable about sexual activity. For children, this discussion would also include a discussion of when sexual activity is permissible; the use of the stick figure chart is useful here. Other people disassociate from their bodies by self-harming (for example, cutting, suicide attempts), or developing panic attacks or eating disorders.

While it is well established that people with learning difficulties are especially vulnerable to sexual violence, the effects on them have been less well studied, possibly because most of our knowledge comes from adult survivor stories and the stories of people with learning difficulties have not been systematically gathered. One small study (O'Callaghan et al, 2003) shows that the impact on victims and families is profound and long lasting, with this group of people suffering additional difficulties including:

- self-harming – this is a relatively common reaction to sexual violence but with this group of people it can also take the form of soiling, which may not receive a sympathetic response from carers;
- a loss of specific skills, such as verbal language, or a more general regression;
- the development of challenging behaviours;
- limited formal support, other than psychiatric treatment, after serious mental health problems develop. It is worth noting here that young women with a combination of learning difficulties and mental illness are the most violent group of people in special hospitals;
- more restrictions in their daily lives as parents and carers become ultra-cautious.

Some people suffer the effects of sexual violence in secret all their lives so it is important for the social worker to be aware of this possibility whatever the social care setting. For example, palliative care tends to operate in a 'culture of niceness' that does not allow for unpleasant experiences to be discussed. Wright (2003) found that a person's imminent death, or the death of a partner who had been sexually violent, meant that they could see that the abuse would soon be over and this broke the silence they had maintained for a lifetime. For example, one woman said: 'Dying will be such a relief for me from him. It is a comfort to know that I haven't done anything wrong, that is wasn't my fault'. Wright makes a powerful plea for palliative care providers to be open to women's stories of distress. Whenever decisions are taken to admit a person to residential care, it is helpful to be sensitive to undisclosed sexual violence; for example, an elderly couple may not wish to live together or residential staff may dread caring for an elderly person whom they know to have been sexually violent earlier in life.

Men who are victims of sexual assault describe their difficulties in being able to acknowledge what has happened and in talking about this with others. The fear of being seen as 'weak' and 'unmanned' is a strong feeling that inhibits seeking help, as well as concern at the reaction they will face from people they know and the authorities ('Will I be believed?', 'Will they think I am gay?', 'What does it say about my sexuality?'). Traditional masculinities do not allow much space for vulnerability; thus the act of sexual violence can severely attack a man's sense of identity, and this is the case for men who consider themselves either straight or gay. A useful website offering information and support services can be accessed at www.male-rape.org.uk, including accounts from victims about their experiences.

Other people who are likely to remain silent are gay and lesbian victims of sexual assault, particularly where it involves a same-sex partner. For gay men, there are difficulties in talking about sexual violence, as there are cultural stigmas around masculinity and penetration, and lesbians have to face an enormous sense of disappointment and disillusionment at having been sexually assaulted by another woman (Walsh, 1999). An important facet of gay affirmative social work is a sensitivity to lesbian and gay people's feelings of shame and disappointment when their relationships become abusive; these, says Walsh, possibly include the loss of a dream that gay would turn out better than straight, or fighting negative messages about the 'inevitable' failure of same-sex relationships, and a reluctance to disclose problems to others.

Black adult victims of sexual violence are also less likely to report their experiences to the police on the grounds that they are less likely to be believed or taken seriously or, where the offender is also black, that they do not wish to fuel public perceptions of black sexuality.

Parmar et al (2005) call for extra support and wider provision of appropriate refuge facilities. This does not mean that you necessarily have to campaign for refuges for each ethnic group; the authors of this book found that raising the issue of minority refuge needs with a local Women's Aid group resulted in small-scale provision, such as specialised lodgings, where black or lesbian or gay people would feel safe.

Further reading

Davies, D. and Neal, C. (eds) (1999) *Pink Therapy: A Guide for Counsellors and Therapists Working with Lesbian, Gay and Bisexual Clients*, Buckingham: Open University Press.

Hawkes, D., Marsh, T.I. and Wilgosh, R. (1998) *Solution Focused Therapy: A Handbook for Health Care Professionals*, Oxford: Butterworth Heinemann.

Selekman, M.D. (2002) *Living on the Razor's Edge. Solution-oriented Brief Family Therapy with Self-harming Adolescents*, London and New York, NY: W.W. Norton.

Summary

- People respond to sexual violence in individual and varied ways.
- Sexual violence can also be complicated by relationships between the victim and the offender.
- Assumptions about how the violence has affected people and how to respond to it, based on group aggregates, need to be treated with caution.
- Listening to the person sensitively is central to good practice.
- Social pressures can affect the experience of sexual violence and these require acknowledgement.

EIGHT

Traditional practices in working with offenders

Sexual offending has become increasingly recognised as a harmful, damaging and common behaviour that crosses boundaries of race, class, age, ability and gender. Nash (1999, p 1) described the 1990s as 'the decade of the predatory sex offender, at least in terms of constructing a demon. Across the world a range of legislation has been set in place which seeks to single out this group of offenders for greater punishment, fewer rights and potential exclusion from society'. Debates abound about the prevalence and nature of this behaviour, with clarion calls for action that have included castration, incarceration and exclusion. 'Paedophile' has become a playground term of abuse, constructing a new folk-devil that can generate huge anxiety, anger and retributive action that is unique to this offending. Sexual offences cover a vast range of behaviours that are defined within their time and culture, with different behaviours being illegal in different countries and developments in legislation to reflect changing social attitudes. For example, despite popular images of the Victorian era as being sexually prudish, the age of consent to sexual intercourse for girls was 12 for most of the 19th century until the Criminal Law Amendment Act of 1885 raised it to 16.

Thomas (2005) provides a comprehensive outline of the development of policy and legislative responses to sex crime in the UK, highlighting the increased concern about sexual misbehaviour and the ways in which governments have attempted to deal with changing public and professional understandings of this. Legislation had been piecemeal and somewhat fragmented until the Sexual Offences Act of 2003 reviewed and codified much of the previous relevant law to bring it into line with current socially acceptable mores. Key changes were established, for example, abolishing specific same-sex offences by subsuming these into the same framework as other-sex offences. Any sexual activity with a child under the age of 16 is potentially criminal, but further restrictions were placed on people in a position of trust with children. Teachers, social workers and so on cannot enter into sexual relationships with young people they know under the age of 18, legislation developed in order to acknowledge young people's potential vulnerability (2003 Sexual Offences Act, Sections 16-24). New offences were created to reflect changes in understanding and technology, so the term 'grooming' to describe preparing a child for sexual abuse was used in the legislation, as well as the codification of offences that were based on the misuse of the internet (for useful information on the nature, prevalence and ways of responding to internet abuse, see Calder, 2004).Voyeurism has become a clearer sexual offence, as well as trafficking people for sexual exploitation. The rapidity of legislative change in this area has been influenced by changing understandings of the nature of sexual violence. For example, concerns about the impact of pornography on those using it and on those who are often forced to take part in its production have led to proposals to make extreme pornography illegal (Home Office, 2006c). There remains little direct evidence that pornography is a causal factor in sexual violence, but there are debates about the way in which this may provide desensitisation to acts that are harmful.

The question of why people commit sexual offences has been subject to a wide range of explanations, including biological, psychological and social answers. Sexual offenders are predominantly men (Grubin, 1998) and this has encouraged explanations based on sexual drive, social learning about masculinity and the abuse of male power. The construction of the paedophile has tended to view sexual offenders as different to other people, creating a type of person who has certain characteristics that are abnormal. The assumption here is that most people (men) are normal and do not sexually offend, nor do they have the inclination to do so. Feminist theorists have raised questions about this construction of difference. For example, Kelly (1996) argued that conceptualising those who commit sexual offences as radically abnormal leads to a pathological perception of individual men that does not address structural male power. In this critique it is more helpful to think of sexual offending as a continuum of the use of male power, with sexual violence being an extreme element of the ways in which men claim and maintain their authority in society and in relationships with women and children. Jenkins (1990) identified that assumptions based on the psychological difference of sexual offenders could lead to practices that ignored social influences and treated the person aggressively and disrespectfully, using power in ways that reinforced the gendered distribution of this. Applying understandings and practices that do not challenge gendered power relations views the person as the problem and allows us to avoid asking the wider questions about male social dominance.

Identifying the prevalence of sexual offences is problematic for a number of reasons, not least the changing ways in which we define them and the difficulties in gaining hard information. The reporting of sexual crime is subject to the same instability as other crime figures, as there are many offences committed that are not reported. Others are investigated and not solved or pursued for lack of evidence and some are prosecuted but fail to gain a conviction. The Home Office produces statistics on crime and demonstrates some of these problems (Walker et al, 2006). There were 52,100 recorded sexual offences in 2003/04 and 60,900 in 2004/05, an increase of 17%. Yet the majority of this increase can be accounted for by the changes in the 2003 Sexual Offences Act, which recategorised indecent exposure as a sexual offence. Under the 2003/04 counting rules, 9,507 indecent exposures had been identified, and in 2004/05 these offences now moved into the sexual offences category, making an apparently huge increase in sexual offending due to an administrative change. The same statistics demonstrated an apparent increase in the number of rapes reported against women, but this may indicate an increased confidence in reporting crime rather than any 'real' increase in the prevalence of rape. As sexual crime is fraught with personal and public shame and is often perpetrated in secrecy, it is almost impossible to gain any absolute truth about the figures. However, combined with the testimony of victims, the figures do tell us that sexual offending is common, does impact hugely on people and requires taking seriously.

Although sexual offenders are predominantly men, the research is unclear about how large this majority is. Duncan and Williams (1998), based on a review of research, estimated that between 76% and 99% of such offenders were male. This leaves questions about the nature and prevalence of women who sexually offend, and the percentage of women offenders seems to be increasing as research develops, perhaps indicating a greater willingness to recognise that women can act in ways that are sexually aggressive. Presuming that offenders are mainly men reflects current knowledge, but may also inhibit the identification of women's abusive sexual behaviour. Theorising women's sexual misbehaviour has been problematic, often doubly damning them for the acts themselves and for transgressing expected gender roles. Women do seem capable of abusing their power and inflicting harm on others, but we have encountered practices that assume that these women have been coerced by adult men into this behaviour, seeking reasons/ excuses that would not be countenanced for men. Saradjian (1996) found that women were capable of acting on their own with attitudes and values that were similar to men who offended, although they were prone to being diagnosed as having mental health problems as it was hard for professionals to conceive of 'normal' women committing sexual offences.

Sexual offending is not the preserve of adults. Hackett (2004) found that up to 20% of all sexual offending was committed by young people between the ages of 10 and 18, with a range of behaviours that mirrored those of adults. Sexually abusive behaviours can be exhibited by even younger children, but as the age of criminal responsibility is 10 these do not appear on official criminal statistics. The reporting of such behaviour by children and young people can be influenced by perceptions that this is a normal part of growing up, that it does not warrant intervention and that responding to it may make things worse, or by confusion about what to do with these children. Of course, it is possible that children and young people are more likely to be reported than adults, as they are policed more heavily through carers and schools and are less sophisticated in their attempts to hide their offending (Myers, 2002). Hackett et al (2003) identified a number of services across the UK and Ireland that have developed to respond specifically to these children, using a range of different approaches to understand, engage and intervene to address the behaviour.

Risk assessment of sexual offenders

Government guidance on the risk assessment and management of sexual offenders has developed in the light of increasing recognition and concern about the prevalence and nature of sexual offences. In 2004, the National Probation Directorate produced a *Sex Offender Strategy for the National Probation Service* that identified four strategic objectives to protect the public from sexual offenders living in the community. These were:

1. Timely assessment using evidenced based tools.
2. Interventions to reduce risk.
3. Interventions to manage risk.
4. Developing accommodation options commensurate to the assessed risk (p 1).

Assessment protocols and specific interventions were incorporated to provide effective management of those who had committed sexual offences, including the development of Multi Agency Public Protection Arrangements to coordinate the activities of the various agencies involved, increasingly through the Multi Agency Public Protection Panel system.

Assessment of sexual offending has tended to follow the dominant and favoured approaches in working with problematic behaviour in general, identifying risks that are located within the individual and their ecological networks. Underpinning this approach has been a strong normative drive based on the identification of risk factors of those people already known to have exhibited harmful behaviour and correlating these against the new subject. Based on this structure, the known risk factors can be identified and charted to produce insight into the relative dangerousness of the person and to indicate the required intervention. This actuarial-type approach has led to assessment protocols and checklists that can be applied by workers to generate insight into the presenting problematic sexual behaviour.

This approach has been subject to criticism, including the lack of acknowledgement of the theoretical bias of the identified risk factors; the denial of the importance of process in the gathering of such facts; the danger that pre-existing lists may not include issues pertinent to the new subject; and the demoting of professional judgement into 'tick-box' practice (Corby, 2000; Parton and O'Byrne, 2000; Fook, 2002; Silver and Miller, 2002). This imposition of external constructs immediately placed the worker as an 'expert' and the person is fitted into broad categories, rather than having any sense of agency within this. Comparisons can be made with existing research in child protection. For example, Goddard et al (1999, p 254), in their critique of structured risk assessments, state:

> Child protection workers are not attempting to predict the behaviour of groups of parents or groups of families. They are required to know which particular abusive parent will abuse which particular child, when and in what circumstances.

This is the case with people with sexually harmful behaviours, where a particular person is being assessed in a particular context, rather than the group to which they have been assigned through a part of their overall behaviour. The local and specific knowledge so crucial in developing change has a tendency to be overlooked or marginalised in this discourse. The inevitable focus on deficits and problems also creates a one-sided assessment that generates its own iatrogenic outcomes by concentrating almost exclusively on what Turnell and Edwards (1999, p 49) called 'the darkest valleys and gloomiest hollows' of family life.

Sexual offenders are a varied and diverse group of people who transgress sexual boundaries regardless of class, race and ability, and assessing their dangerousness is important for the well-being of others and indeed themselves. Due to the heterogeneous nature of this group of offenders, there is no current consistent profile of the sex offender (Craig et al, 2005). There has been much research into trying to understand what leads people to sexually offend and in how to respond effectively to this, with large studies exploring the characteristics of those who have offended and who have gone on to reoffend. This research has been hampered by the fact that reoffending following identification is remarkably low, which is contrary to popular (and many professional) expectations (Grubin, 1998). Indeed, trying to establish who has reoffended is problematic, as there are difficulties in reporting, recording and convicting for sexual offences. Corbett et al (2003) found that 12% of their study sexually reoffended, but that sexual offending can be redefined as violence against the person in the criminal justice process. This phenomenon contributes towards the low base rate of sexual reconviction (Soothill et al, 2000).

This has meant that identifying characteristics of the small group of people who *reoffend* has limited application to the wider offending population, as the number is not robust enough for definitive answers. Thus much of the work has been focused on those who have offended, seeking to develop typologies and to understand what makes sexual offenders *different*. These factors are then suggested as indicators of dangerousness; usually that the more factors there are, the more dangerous a person is. This approach assumes that there is such an entity as a sexual offender (or types of sexual offender) that can be discovered through the investigation of the factors.

As in many risk assessment approaches, these factors can be classified as 'static' or 'dynamic'; that is, they are fixed or susceptible to change. Meta-analyses of recidivism studies of men who sexually offend (where the same factors come up in many independent studies) show that the strongest predictors are as follows:

- deviant sexual interests;
- has committed a variety of sexual crimes;
- began offending at an early age – although this finding is not supported by research into young sexual offenders; most young sexual offenders are not at high risk of developing into adult offenders (Worling and Curwen, 2000);
- has targeted boys, strangers or unrelated victims;
- sexual interest in children (the single strongest predictor).

After this, the next most important predictors are:

- prior offences;
- age (youth);
- antisocial personality disorder.

'Deviance' is a term that requires some consideration, as it can have different meanings depending on who is making the judgement. However, it is generally taken to mean sexual interests that are illegal and inappropriate, for example, an interest in sexual violence or in children. As can be seen, all these are static factors, and indeed most identified factors within such protocols are highly stable. There are *no* well-established dynamic risk predictors. Static factors are useful for assessing enduring propensities to reoffend but they are unhelpful in constructing treatment plans and cannot be used to assess treatment outcomes or to monitor risk on community supervision:

> There are no validated scales for assessing changes in the risk of sexual offence recidivism, therefore the available information is better at identifying high-risk offenders than it is at determining how to intervene, or whether interventions have been successful. (Hanson, 2004, p 40)

We can say that someone who has behaved badly in the past, has done this several times in different ways and reports an interest in illegal sexual activity is at high risk of future offending, but does it really take a formal risk assessment protocol to lead us to this fairly obvious conclusion? In addition to this, the predictive accuracy of most actuarial tools is rather modest (Silver and Miller, 2002), despite claims for improved effectiveness over other approaches. For example, Christodoulides et al (2005), when considering the effectiveness of a Risk Assesment Matrix for adolescents, found that it was not possible to distinguish recidivists from non-recidivists, as there were too many variations to establish a definite pattern.

Some of the risk factors do change as more research becomes available. The image of someone who is socially inept is not borne out by the evidence. Sex offenders do not display a general deficit in emotional functioning and it is not known whether any emotional deficits are offence-specific or whether offenders use their emotional intelligence for maladaptive purposes (Puglia et al, 2005).

Denial has been viewed as a factor in increased risk. However, denial of the offence is not correlated with an increased risk of reconviction

(Hanson and Bussière, 1998). Denial serves to block the realisation of the severity of the behaviour, its impact on the victim and the potential consequences for offenders. Denying the offence may well be linked to family dynamics – protecting family members from stress and/or self from emotional rejection. It buys time for offender and family to adjust to the idea and reality of the consequences of the behaviour. Excluding deniers from treatment is unwarranted, as there is little evidence of the effect of denial on treatment outcome. Deniers are more able to relax and participate in discussion if they do not fear being tricked into a confession (Cooper, 2005).

Interventions

Both government guidance and most practice handbooks favour a particular theoretical approach to responding to sexual violence – that of cognitive behavioural therapy. The Prison Service and National Probation Service have a joint approach to sexual offenders (National Probation Directorate, 2002) that includes the Sex Offender Treatment Programme. All programmes are accredited for use by the Correctional Services Accreditation Panel based on an evidence-informed decision. The cognitive behavioural approach is explained as teaching 'offenders to understand and control thinking, feelings and behaviour'. The accredited programmes in the prison and the community:

* share the same treatment model;
* use cognitive behavioural methods;
* target the same dynamic risk factors;
* have similar selection criteria;
* are suitable for all forms of sex offending;
* are groupwork rather than individual programmes (National Probation Directorate, 2002, p 4).

Box 8.1: Description of a Sex Offender Groupwork Programme (C-SOGP)

This programme has three main components:

Induction Module

This is a 50-hour module designed as the main point of entry into the programme. Offenders will start this module if they have been sentenced from Court to attend as part of a 3-year Community Rehabilitation Order. Offenders released from prison who have not previously taken part in a treatment programme will also start the C-SOGP in the Induction Module. The Induction Module is a closed group (i.e. all group members start the programme together and no new members join the group once it has started). The first week of the Module is a 5-day block. Following this first week the Module continues in two-and-a-half-hour sessions. These sessions are usually delivered on a weekly basis for ten weeks. Some Probation Areas may run this Module on a twice-weekly basis or run two sessions on one day. The Module aims to help offenders take greater personal responsibility for their offence and to reduce the minimisation often found in offender accounts. During the course of the Module, offenders will be encouraged to identify patterns in their offending behaviour.

Long Term Therapy Programme

Following completion of the Induction Module, offenders who are assessed as Medium and High Risk or High Deviance, will be entered into the Long Term programme. Offenders who have completed treatment in prison but who are still assessed as High Risk and/or Deviance will usually enter the CSOGP in the Long Term programme. This contains six modules and the offender may enter at the start of any Module (other than Victim Empathy). The Long Term programme is usually run on weekly basis of one session per week. The total number of 190 hours worked in this part of the C-SOGP will take seventy-six weeks to complete if the programme is run on a weekly basis. These modules are designed to continue the process of

- challenging distorted thinking
- identifying maladaptive relationship styles and core beliefs
- learning new skills to improve self-management
- understanding the role that deviant fantasy plays in offending and techniques to control such fantasies
- developing victim empathy, relapse prevention skills and new lifestyle goals.

> Research suggests that it is inadvisable for sex offenders to commence treatment unless they are able to complete the programme. Therefore sentencers are recommended to use Sec 58, PCCS Act 2000 to apply extended sentence provision of 3 year post release supervision periods for sex offender cases.
>
> The Treatment Manager will make a judgement of suitability for the programme in cases of shorter licence periods.
>
> **50-Hour Relapse Prevention Programme**
> Offenders who have been assessed as Low Risk and Deviance following completion of the Induction Module will complete the 50-hour RP Programme. Offenders who have made treatment gains during successful completion of the sex offending treatment programme in prison, and who are assessed as Low/ Medium risk and Low Deviance may enter the C-SOGP in the 50-Hour RP programme. This is run as a rolling programme; therefore, offenders can enter at any session and continue their attendance for twenty weeks. This programme is designed for offenders whose behaviour may be less entrenched or who can build on treatment gains made elsewhere. The programme includes work on
>
> * challenging distortions
> * victim empathy
> * relapse prevention and
> * lifestyle change.
>
> *Source:* National Probation Directorate, 2002, p 13.

Cognitive behavioural approaches assume that the person has 'deviant' sexual arousal, which is supported by distorted thinking about the impact of their actions, particularly on the victim, plus social skills deficits that contribute to a cycle of abusive behaviour. Within this cycle there are certain beliefs and ways of thinking that support the build-up to the offence, providing justifications for their abuse. Following the abusive act, people are unlikely to be caught, thus avoiding any negative consequences of their actions. This reinforces the desire and motivation to repeat the behaviour, with certain triggers in this cycle that can be identified (Beckett, 1994). Denial or minimisation of the harm done is expected in this model, as this is part of the distorted thinking patterns. It is similar to a model of addiction, where people become locked into patterns of behaviour that are unhelpful. Key elements of the cycle are the focus of intervention, with efforts to change these to break down the abusive patterns. The underlying assumption is that the person, for reasons of upbringing or culture, has developed *wrong* ways of thinking and acting that require correction. Illegal sexual fantasies are viewed as having a major role in supporting the behaviour, so there is an emphasis on finding these and changing them. This can be achieved through using images to ascertain sexual interest and also by using the 'penile plethysmograph', a technology that measures sexual arousal in the penis by reactions to visual or audio stimulus. Brown (2005) outlines the development and practice of cognitive behavioural programmes for sexual offenders, including the various methods employed.

Challenging the person directly and forcefully about their beliefs is a common practice technique, including using groupwork. This has led some practitioners to raise questions about the ways in which such an approach can result in oppressive practices that may simply reinforce notions of force and power (Jenkins, 1990). For example, by *breaking down* denial and minimisation there is a danger that offenders may feel subjected to aggressive techniques that reinforce their own use of power in their relationships. Rather than questioning the basis of the use of power, such approaches enforce and reinforce traditional notions of power as coercive. There are difficulties in inviting people to consider how they can change their use of power, when they are faced with approaches that seem to be based on aggression and enforcement.

Claims made for cognitive behavioural approaches are global in their scope, allegedly providing the answer for *all* sexual offending. However, the evidence for this is not as definitive as its adherents sometimes claim. Recent research raises doubts about the effectiveness of confrontational conventional cognitive behavioural programmes that focus exclusively on sexual offending (Polaschek, 2001; Vivian-Byrne, 2002). Such an approach has been shown to be of limited effectiveness with young sexual offenders (for an overview of the research, see Hackett, 2004). Follow-up outcome studies show that it is wise to treat any early apparent successes with caution given the incrementally disappointing reconviction rate indicators that have emerged over time (Mair, 2004). For example, the initial research into pre-accredited cognitive skills programmes revealed 14% lower reconviction rates than comparison groups (Friendship, 2002), but this has not been echoed by subsequent research findings. An evaluation of accredited cognitive skills programmes for adult prisoners found no differences in reconviction rates (Falshaw et al, 2003); neither were there any differences between reconviction rates of adult men and young offenders who started custodially based cognitive skills programmes (Cann et al, 2003).

Despite the intensive nature of the programmes offered, there is actually little evidence that long-term interventions work. Research about the effectiveness of therapy in general has found that increasing the number of therapy sessions is not always associated with better outcomes and desired outcomes actually decelerate as the number of sessions increases (Lambert and Ogles, 2004; Orlinsky et al, 2004). Some abusive adolescents have therapeutic needs that are not addressed by offence-specific or offence-related group treatment programmes (Richardson, 2005). What works better seems to be community-based supervision, where support can be offered to increase desistance by helping overcome difficulties such as family problems, employment and so on (Farrall, 2004). This seems to indicate that it would be helpful to move away from the current dominance of cognitive behavioural programmes to customised, relationship-oriented practice.

Sexual offending and people with learning difficulties

There has been concern at the over-representation of people with learning disabilities among those identified as sexual offenders, leading in some cases to the presence of learning disabilities as a risk factor in assessment protocols. Some specialist provision has been created for people with learning disabilities; however, the research has raised some broader questions about this. The existing literature suggests that learning disability remains a poorly defined condition; as such, the interpretation of problem sexual behaviours in people with learning difficulties relies on broad, at times vague, definitions. No research finds cognitive distortions to be key factors in the behaviour (Tudway and Darmoody, 2005). In some studies, sexual recidivism in this group is both higher and occurs within a shorter period of time than in non-disabled groups. Offender characteristics include:

- inattention (poor ability to tune in and recognise what is important) – combated by providing limited amounts of information, looking at the person directly and using practical examples;
- lack of perception (poor ability to maker sense of and understand information) – combated by using multiple sensory information, explaining clearly and simply and allowing frequent opportunities to practice;
- poor memory (poor ability to acquire, hold and retrieve information) – combated by limiting amount of information

presented, using short chunks of information and giving visual prompts to jog the memory;

- limited comprehension (poor ability to understand what is being said) – combated by reducing the speed of what is said, modifying language used, clarifying complex ideas and continually repeating and rephrasing key learning points;
- difficulties in expressing themselves (poor ability to communicate messages to other people) – combated by using symbols, pictures and drawings to help explain complex concepts such as emotions and thoughts;
- poor ability to cope with change – combated by keeping changes to the minimum;
- poor ability to practise self-control techniques cognitively, and a need for longer timescales and more external controls – combated by frequent repetition of simple information until assimilated and principles applied to a variety of contexts.

Sex offenders with learning difficulties have a higher incidence of family discord, psychosocial deprivation, behavioural disturbances at school, psychiatric illness, social and sexual naivety, poor ability to form normal sexual and personal relationships, and poor impulse control. Some offenders' behaviour can be classified as less 'deviant' when considered in the context of the individual's developmental level – it may be age-appropriate in terms of the usual sexual development of children. This group of offenders generally make little progress on mainstream programmes regarding sexual interests and attitudes to offending (Craig and Hutchinson, 2005).

Chelsea is a 15-year-old girl who was made the subject of a care order three years ago following severe neglect. Her first two foster placements broke down because of her sexually concerning behaviour with other foster children. She has been in her current placement for 18 months. Her foster mother is concerned about her physically and sexually abusive behaviour with toddlers. Chelsea is also causing concern at school by being sexually aggressive towards boys. She has a statement of educational needs and is struggling in mainstream education.

Create a plan that will ensure the safety of Chelsea, her foster siblings and fellow pupils. Taking into account Chelsea's learning difficulties, how will you involve her in making this plan successful?

Further reading

Brown, S. (2005) *Treating Sex Offenders: An Introduction to Sex Offender Treatment Programmes*, Cullompton: Willan.

Milner, J. and Myers, S. (2007) *Working with Violence: Risk, Safety and Responsibility*, Basingstoke: Palgrave.

Summary

- Sexual offences and abusive behaviours are committed by a wide range of people; there is no typical offender.
- Sexual offenders have become the focus of increased cultural, legal and professional interest.
- It is difficult to be absolute about the levels of risk posed by individual sexual offenders.
- Research in this area remains at an early stage.
- Public and professional perceptions of sexual offenders are often not supported by evidence.
- Cognitive behavioural models of understanding sexual violence are dominant, but are not robustly supported by evidence.

NINE

Newer practices in working with offenders

Given the current anxieties about sexual offenders, attempting to work in ways that are creative and meaningful can be limited. Assessment and practices that are dominated by presumptions of cognitive deficits are of limited demonstrated effectiveness, despite claims to the contrary. The authors have worked with children, young people and adults using the following assessment and intervention approaches for people who have harmful sexual behaviours. These are considered to be useful and effective alternative ways of working.

Developing a 'Signs of Safety' assessment

Assessment underpinned by solution-focused (De Shazer, 1988) and narrative (White and Epston, 1990) principles and practices has been found to be useful in producing a good understanding of sexual offenders and the ways in which they can be assisted in developing lives that are free of the problematic sexual behaviour. The aim of the assessment is to determine the level of intervention required to assist the person in maintaining a future that is free of sexually concerning or harmful behaviour. The following goals have been developed by The Junction, a Barnardo's children's service:

- To be specific about the detail of the alleged sexually harmful behaviour.
- To clarify what everyone understands about the behaviour and their individual levels of concern (offender, family, victim, agency).
- To consider how the behaviour has already been responded to.
- To identify what works in assisting the offender to avoid the sexually concerning behaviour.
- To agree a strategy for maintaining a problem-free future and to develop safety.
- To establish the motivation and ability of participants to work towards safety.

Listening to professional stories

Referring agencies to Barnardo's The Junction service include the courts (often for psychiatric and psychological assessment), social services, the probation service and youth offending teams. Their information is helpful in considering how people perceive and make sense of the problem. The referral tends to be presented in ways that focus on problems, be they sexual behaviour, educational experiences, family difficulties or previous history. At this stage of the referral, it is important to ask questions about the strengths of the offender, to enable a clearer picture to emerge but also to engage the referrer in reflection on their 'richer' understanding of the situation. The referrer is asked about their hopes and how The Junction can best help the agency *and* the offender. A key question is: 'What would you need to be different as a result of work with The Junction?'. Detail is sought, rather than accepting broad categorisations such as 'conduct disorder', 'attention deficit hyperactive disorder (ADHD)', 'learning difficulties', 'autism spectrum disorder', 'personality disorder', 'impulsivity', 'sexualised behaviour', 'dysfunctional' or 'acting out', all common contemporary labels. This allows for the identification of the specific behaviours that have led to these labels and enables the development of a clearer picture of the individual person in their context. Applying such labels to people can have the unintended consequence of reducing the capacity for change, as they can provide a ready-made reason for minimising personal responsibility ('It's because of my/his ADHD/personality disorder' and so on). For example, Nylund (2000) specifically addresses the consequences and complexities of ADHD, identifying the problems such a diagnosis can generate.

Kayleigh is a young single mother with a three-year-old daughter who is the subject of a residence order to her maternal grandmother. Kayleigh is currently in a relationship with a 49-year-old man who served a three-year prison sentence for sexually abusing his stepdaughter. Kayleigh is eight months pregnant with his child.

You have been asked to undertake a pre-birth risk assessment. Kayleigh tells you that her new partner is willing to do anything to be allowed to keep this child. What would he have to be doing differently (be specific) for you to be confident that he would be safe with the child?

Practice principles

The practice principles of the Signs of Safety approach outlined by Turnell and Edwards (1999) have been helpful in developing an assessment process, particularly where there are concerns about the safety of others within the household. These include:

- understanding the position of each family member;
- finding exceptions to the problem;
- discovering family strengths and resources;
- focusing on goals;
- scaling safety and progress;
- assessing willingness, confidence and capacity.

Understanding the position of each family member

Interviews with offenders can take place in many settings, at home, in prison or at the office, but the common thread is to have a purposeful, engaging and productive meeting that can in itself be helpful to the person and family. Given the concerns about violence, it may well be that the offender has been removed from their home or that children have been removed for their safety. In developing safety, it is important to consider the views of all family members if they are to remain together in a violence-free environment.

To enable family members to actively take part in the process and to understand their position(s) on the behaviour, solution-focused questions are used. These include:

- How did they think we could help?
- What do they think the problem is?
- What do they think is the reason for this problem behaviour?
- What effect has the problem behaviour had on each family member?
- How has the behaviour impacted on the victim(s)?
- How has the problem changed things for the family members?
- How have you coped with the violence and its consequences?
- How has the violence been successfully managed in the past?
- What would be helpful in developing safety now?

The offender will be asked about their understanding of the behaviour or event using similar questions, including:

- What impact has the problem behaviour had on you and your family?
- How good is your life following the problem?
- When has your life been at its best – what was happening?
- Who has been most helpful to you following the problem – what did they do?
- Who is worried about your behaviour – how do they show this?

Further questions can be aimed at understanding the offender's view of the victim, for example:

- How have things changed for the victim?
- How do you think the behaviour has impacted on them?
- How good was your relationship with the victim before the violence?
- How has your behaviour changed your relationship with the victim?

Each of these questions can be elaborated on for detail using the solution-focused technique of asking 'what', 'where', 'when', 'who' and 'how' questions, but never 'why' questions as these tend to limit responses. Within this approach, there is a minimum of emphasis on exploring causality. This is a contested area of little agreement even within the professional literature, and it is not always necessary to understand the causes in order to develop solutions to the problem (Wittgenstein, 1963). In considering why something has happened, it is likely that the person asking the question will already have decided on their preferred theoretical explanation and focus on substantiating this, thus limiting the specific local knowledge of the subject (Sinclair et al, 1995). For example, if an interviewer holds that the notion of cognitive distortions is central to explaining sexual misbehaviour, questions will be asked to identify these, and it is likely that they will be found. This phenomenon has been supported by research into risk assessments, whereby the availability of data on risk factors tends to outweigh data on other more protective factors, leading to an overemphasis on the former (Campbell, 2003).

The offender may be invited to name the problem, an externalising technique developed in narrative therapy that allows for separation of the person from the problem (White and Epston, 1990). This is counter to many therapeutic approaches that view behaviours as indicating a truth of the person. Rather than seeing the behaviour as an intrinsic and fixed part of their being, located within distorted ways of thinking or dysfunctional personality constructs, this approach views behaviour as something that can be modified by distancing people from it. This allows them to consider the behaviour as an entity to be tackled through reconfiguring their relationship with it. For example, a young person named their sexually abusive behaviour as 'the Touching Monster', and the worker and the child were able together to explore this monster, identifying what it liked and disliked, when it was strong, what supported it, who was good or bad for it and where it lived in order to understand the nature of the problem better (Myers et al, 2003). When this became clearer, strategies emerged from the understanding of the young person (who is the expert on the 'monster') to reduce the influence of the behaviour in their lives. This has the potential to have more personal meaning for the young person, rather than imposing an external construct such as a cognitive behavioural 'cycle of abuse' model, the limitations of which have been identified elsewhere (Hackett, 2000). In assessment, this can be a useful tool in identifying and promoting change.

This process of questioning is designed to elicit local understanding of the problem and to begin to identify the ways in which people can work towards managing the problem. Most meetings result in some ability to plan ahead with ideas of how to deal with the behaviour, based on strengths and previous successes in leading a violence-free life.

Exceptions and strengths

Recognising that there will always be exceptions to the behaviour is an important principle of solution-focused work. The violence will only be a part of the overall behaviour of the person. It is helpful to talk very clearly about the times when the violence does not happen and when the offender has behaved in responsible ways. This allows for the detailed exploration of what happens when things are going right in someone's life, when their behaviour is good (or at least non-violent). Such detail can give clues and strategies to assist the offender in doing more of the same. Questions may include:

- When are things okay in the family?
- When is the offender's behaviour non-violent?
- What and who helps you to be the best person you can be?
- When did you have the opportunity to be violent but chose not to – how did this happen?
- When have you demonstrated respect towards other people?

- What good things do other people say about you – when?
- When have you acted responsibly?

This principle can also be applied to exploring the family resources, asking questions such as:

- How have you successfully dealt with problems in the past?
- When have you worked really well together to sort things out?
- When have you been happiest with your relationship?
- What was happening then to make it so good?
- What works best for you and your particular circumstances?

Assisting offenders and families to identify their strengths validates the totality of their experiences, places the current problem behaviour in context, makes contact with professionals less threatening and gives ideas for transferring skills into future safety plans. It can also indicate that safety is difficult to achieve if the offender and family cannot see any strengths that can be built on to use in the future.

Mohammed has served a prison sentence for raping his niece when he was 16. He is due for release and you are part of the team undertaking a risk assessment to manage his return to the community.

What conversation could you have with him that would enable him to demonstrate that he has the capacity to behave in respectful and responsible ways? Why would it be important to seek out this information?

It has been recognised that strengths are an important and often neglected part of the equation in understanding people subject to assessment. There have been attempts to identify what are general individual and family strengths and to codify these into checklists that can be matched against further subjects (see, for example, Gilgun, 1999). A solution-focused approach is different from this in that preordained strengths are not seen as necessarily true for the person or family. It is important to seek the particular strengths of that unique person or family, which may be different from the known factors, and, indeed, over-reliance on general checklists may lead to a more optimistic assessment if the meaning of those factors is different for this specific person and their family. We need to remember that one person or family's strength may well be another's weakness (Rutter, 1999).

Focusing on goals

The setting of goals is crucial to the process of assessment, as this enables clarity about the nature of the violence and what can be done about it. The referring agency is invited to be precise about their concerns and goals, stating what they would like to see being done differently by the offender and within what timescale. Given the professional perceptions of violence, it is often difficult for workers to do this, and even when they do there is often a suspicion and lack of confidence in the outcomes.

> Following the discovery that a man had been sexually inappropriate with children when he was younger, there was a child protection investigation into his current family situation that led to his removal from his children. As part of the assessment, the social worker was invited to say what they would like to see him doing for his behaviour with his children to be considered safe. The social worker said that if the man disclosed to his partner and the social worker what had happened in detail, this would be a useful indicator of safety within the family. The man did so, but was then told by the social worker that he was only doing it to get his children back. The children remained separated from their father.
>
> *What more useful goals could you develop in this case?*

A useful consideration identified by Turnell and Edwards (1999) is to ask the agency to think about what would need to be happening for them to be comfortable enough to close the case. Research in child protection has identified the lack of clarity from agencies with offenders and families about what needs to be done as a major point of conflict. Explicit goals from agencies are therefore important in order to be fair to people. When they know what has to be achieved, they can begin to work towards this. Although it may not at first appear so, a useful response from offenders and families is to 'get social services out of their lives', as this opens spaces to negotiate what it would take to do this and how to achieve it.

The use of the 'Miracle Question' is one of the solution-focused tools that has been successful in engaging people about goals (De Shazer, 1988). There are several versions of this, but a suggested format in cases of sexual violence is as follows:

> Imagine that you go to sleep tonight and when you wake
> up in the morning the judge has become convinced that

you are a safe person around women. What will he notice about you that has changed? How would you know things had changed? What would be different? How would your family know things had changed?

This is a creative way of engaging people to consider change, goals and ways of achieving these. Imagining a problem-free future and then tracking back to see how this can be reached gives hope for people who are often struggling with the difficulties of problematic behaviour. The discourses around violence tend to disempower people subjected to them, so generating hope and identifying ways forward are central to an active assessment. A further technique to achieve this is to ask people to imagine several years ahead when they are living their preferred problem-free life. Incremental steps can then be agreed to work towards this. Of course, dreams do not always come true, but it is preferable to work towards these than to remain locked within a nightmare of fixed identities and lack of personal agency.

Asking the offender to be specific about how they are going to keep violence-free encourages a sense of responsibility as well as demonstrating whether they have the capacity and resources to achieve this. There may be a genuine desire to change their behaviour, but this needs to be supported by robust and detailed plans to demonstrate *how* they are going to achieve this; plans that can be measured and verified.

Scaling safety and progress

The Junction has utilised charts developed by Turnell and Edwards (1999) that assist in representing circumstances, concerns and strengths. These allow for the identification of concerns and strengths as well as the action required to achieve agreed goals. The principle behind these is one of developing safety. This is viewed as more than an absence of problems; it is about an increase in positive, safe behaviour. It is difficult to demonstrate that you have stopped doing something, particularly in the construction of violence, which has a tendency to locate the problem as part of a personality trait. It is more useful to demonstrate over time that you are doing things that indicate safety. This is actually a harder task than simply not doing something, as it requires more than a passive absence. It requires a positive demonstration of the person's safe behaviour and an increase in reasonable responsibility taking. Rather than waiting for something not to happen, it is more helpful to develop constructive actions that demonstrate a willingness and ability to change over time, evaluated through specific agreed goals.

Figure 9.1 comprises two forms. One is completed based on assessments undertaken in The Junction to illustrate how it can be used. The young person is a composite of various cases to demonstrate how safety needs to be at the forefront when dealing with potentially harmful behaviour. The second is blank to allow you to complete this for someone you may be working with where safety is of concern.

The concerns and dangers are listed to be explicit about the views of all parties and to enable the offender and their family to be clear about the agency's worries. The concerns/dangers can include all factors that people consider to be worrying, including the actual behaviour, attitudes to it, limitations to change and current and future potential for repetition. The choice of the terms 'concerns' and 'dangers' as opposed to 'risk' is a conscious one that recognises the contested nature of the risk concept (Ward and Wolverton, 1990; Goddard et al, 1999). Undertaking a 'risk assessment' has the potential to dwell solely on the dangers, therefore a Signs of Safety approach is more interested in developing safety, recognising the limitations of claims made by structured risk assessment models (Houston and Griffiths, 2000).

Safety is explored and those elements that are felt to be positive are identified and listed. There may be ambivalence about some of the factors, or they may be strengths in some contexts and concerns in others. This should be made explicit and the concerns–safety axis can be seen as a continuum, rather than an either/or situation. The level of concern or comfort with each of the factors can be scaled to determine people's perceptions of them, using a simple 0 to 10 scale, where 0 is of no concern and 10 is the maximum concern, or 0 is low safety and 10 is high safety. This allows for comparisons to be made between the perceptions of various actors in the process. It allows the offender and their family to clearly locate the concerns of the professionals involved and invites professionals to justify their concerns. The focus is on enabling detail to emerge through the application of further exploratory questioning of all parties. The list is not prescribed nor exclusively based on pre-existing professional or theoretical knowledge, but enables local knowledge and circumstances to be made visible.

The offender is invited to take part in the process and to give their views, which reduces the potential for conflict and destructive disagreement. Messages about the fixed nature of the violent offender, focusing on that behaviour as their defining characteristic, denies their complexity and gives space to tell their whole story. This also allows the partners and children to have their feelings heard. They may well

Figure 9.1: Constructing safety plans with people who have harmful sexual behaviours

Name Thomas Jones _____   Date 20th January 2004 _____

CONCERNS	SAFETY		
1. Thomas was sexually abused by his father and a female relative. He tells strangers about this which makes him vulnerable to further abuse.			
2. Thomas touched his brothers and sisters sexually			3. Thomas only has supervised contact with his brothers and sisters
4. Thomas has learning difficulties that make it hard for him to understand how to keep safe			
5. Thomas breaks rules all the time and enjoys doing this.	6. He has agreed to keep all rules. This is as yet untested.		
7. He has urges to touch children sexually			
8. He has been alone with other young kids, even though he knows this is not allowed.			9. Staff are escorting him everywhere
10. He understands what consent is but has been inappropriate with other young people			
11. He is disrespectful to his carers.			
12. His behaviour has been poor when on public transport			13. Staff are taking him to and from college
Child/young person's goals	**Carers' Goals**		**Professionals' Goals**
Thomas wants more freedom to go out with his friends on his own.	Staff want Thomas to be safe enough around children so that he can have more freedom.		Social worker wants Thomas to be safe enough around young children so that he can have more freedom.

STRENGTHS SCALE

Scale the young person's current strengths to control the sexual behaviour

0 = Struggling to control   10 = Back in control

1. Thomas understands that what he did was wrong and how to control his urges but he forgets to do this. He is disrespectful to staff and breaks rules designed for his own safety from allegations all the time. There are no signs of safety other than those imposed in terms of strict supervision.

Signed	Signed	Signed

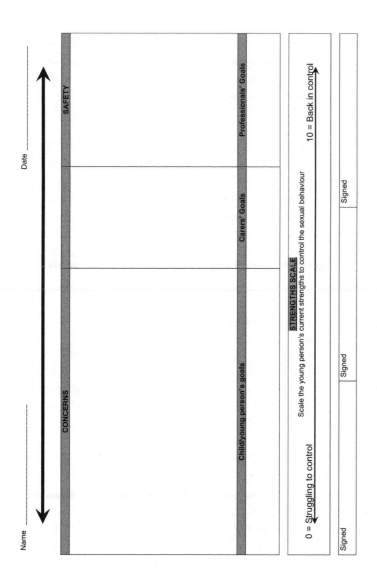

Name _____   Date _____

CONCERNS		SAFETY
Child/young person's goals	Carers' Goals	Professionals' Goals

STRENGTHS SCALE

Scale the young person's current strengths to control the sexual behaviour

0 = Struggling to control   10 = Back in control

Signed _____   Signed _____   Signed _____

love the person but hate the specific violent behaviour and these ambivalences need to be recognised if they are to be fully engaged and respected.

The Signs of Safety approach is a useful tool for monitoring and reviewing progress, as it demands clear actions to achieve the agreed goals underpinned by consideration of the concerns. Appropriate responsibility is spread across all the participants and the initial scaling of concerns can be revisited and reviewed based on specific goals and behaviours. For example, initially people may feel that the violent behaviour is serious at a level of 9 (on a 0–10 scale), but as the offender achieves goals around responsible behaviour, this concern may reduce at further meetings. Conversely, the worker may feel that the offender's engagement is initially at 8, but following failure to attend agreed meetings this may be re-rated at 5. If the family rates their concerns about the behaviour at 8, the offender will be invited to think about what they have to do to reduce that level of concern. This dynamic process minimises the problems associated with anchoring biases (Friedlander and Stockman, 1983), whereby information obtained in the early stages of an assessment is privileged over subsequent information that is inconsistent with this, leading to a rigid construction of the person.

Willingness, confidence and capacity

The agreed goals may be aspirational. It is therefore important to assess how motivated people are to achieve these. Asking how confident different people are (on a scale of 0–10) in achieving the goals can lead to useful indicators about the potential for change. Evidence for these perceptions needs to be made explicit. If the victim is not very confident that these can be achieved, this will indicate an increased danger. Willingness is not static; the worker through their interventions can generate hope and energy to change. A strengths-based approach allows for the identification of skills that may have been hidden or undervalued, thus providing resources to enhance confidence and capacity. Transferring skills from other areas into changing problematic behaviour is a useful solution-focused principle.

Exploring what action has been taken following the violent behaviour will give clues as to the ability to create and sustain plans. What action has the offender taken to change their behaviour? How successful has this been? Offenders may be able to see where they would like to be but may have little idea of how to get there, even with helpful questions. When steps to achieve goals are identified, there may be little confidence from families that the offender can achieve these given their knowledge of them. Despite best intentions, an offender may not have the capacity for sustaining change and their previous attempts may have been unsuccessful.

A worker may be in the position of having to question what evidence there is to support an offender's view that they can change. If there is none, the judgement that the offender is not yet safe should be an open and transparent one, based on tangible actions (or lack of them). Where there are no signs of safety other than those externally imposed, work can usefully be done to increase the offender's acceptance of, and compliance with, monitoring. This process follows the same sequence of work as that outlined above. At one level, this makes the task of the carers/monitors easier. At another level, as the offender becomes more accepting of external controls, they may discover an ability to develop rudimentary internal controls.

Further reading

Hackett, S. (2001) *Facing the Future. A Guide for Parents of Young People who have Sexually Abused*, Lyme Regis: Russell House Publishing.

Jenkins, A. (1990) *Invitations to Responsibility*, Adelaide: Dulwich Centre Publications.

Milner, J. and Myers, S. (2007) *Working with Violence: Practices and Policies in Risk Assessment and Management*, Basingstoke: Palgrave Macmillan.

Turnell, A. and Edwards, S. (1999) *Signs of Safety: A Solution and Safety Oriented Approach to Child Protection Casework*, London and New York, NY: W. W. Norton.

Summary

- Risk is harder to measure than safety.
- Co-constructing safety is a helpful approach for the worker in preventing future violence.
- The focus on the identification of measurable indicators of safety in solution-focused approaches to working with offenders reduces the anxieties inherent in risk assessment and management.

- Using the technique of 'externalising' developed in narrative therapy provides a constructive way of working with offenders who would otherwise be considered in more traditional approaches to be in denial.

TEN

Conclusion

Social workers are placed in the position of having to engage with sexual issues in all their dealings with service users, although this may not be apparent or obvious in some situations. The 'taken-for-granted' assumptions about sex and sexuality that permeate society generally are reflected in the ways in which it is possible to forget, marginalise or discriminate in everyday social work practices, sometimes unwittingly although occasionally intentionally. Broader thinking about sex and sexuality enable social workers to practise *reflexively*, that is, to consider how their actions are producing particular constructions of sex and sexuality that have consequences for people. Being aware that the values and knowledge that social workers bring to making sense of people and their situation at least provides the opportunity to work helpfully, acknowledging that how sex and sexuality are understood does have an impact on people that can often be problematic. Transparency around the conceptualisation of sex and sexuality assists the social worker in being aware of how power operates in privileging some sexualities over others, generating narrow notions of expected sexual behaviour, pathologising differences and reducing complexity to socially influenced artificial categories.

Policies and guidance abound in the broad arena of sex and sexuality and social workers are increasingly expected to work with these, for example, in sexual health, working with victims and working with offenders. Talking about sex and sexuality can be difficult, although it can also be fascinating and extremely important for those whose opportunities to share their experiences are restricted by social expectations and taboos. The guidance can be contradictory and based on unacknowledged assumptions that limit creative practice and reduce the space to respond to individual needs. Social workers need the skills and knowledge to intervene confidently and effectively to assist people whether this is through broad interventions or where sex and sexuality are of specific concern. This does not have to be *problem-saturated* work; it can be liberating and refreshing to be honest about such matters in a world that tends to judge, allow and silence what can be said.

The authors are particularly concerned with ensuring that social workers have tools that are helpful in their everyday practices, tools that are based on clear knowledge and on the best available evidence. These are not fixed states, and the authors have reflected on the original *Social Work and Sexual Problems* to gain some understanding of how the knowledge base has changed. It was no surprise to find that there have been radical changes in the way we think about sex and sexuality, the language we use, the settings in which sex and sexuality are now commonly engaged with, and the ways in which social workers work with people. Some of these reflect general changes in social work, such as the introduction of postmodern theorising, but many are specific to sex and sexuality, such as the legal and attitudinal changes to same-sex relationships; the influence of a sexually explicit media and culture; the changes in responding to sexual violence; the availability of pornography on the internet; and the development of HIV/AIDS. In the next 20 years there will doubtless be further changes that will provide more challenges for social workers who wish to work effectively and positively with people where sex and sexuality are issues.

References

Age Concern (1996) *HIV and AIDs in Older People*, London: Age Concern.

Age Concern (1989) *Living, Loving and Ageing*, Liverpool: Age Concern/University of Liverpool Institute of Human Ageing.

Allen, C. and Leventhal, B. (1999) 'History, Culture, and Identity: What makes GLBT battering different', in B. Leventhal and S.E. Lundy (eds), *Same-sex Domestic Violence. Strategies for Change*, London: Sage Publications.

Allen, G. A. (1997) 'The double edged sword of genetic determinism: Social and political agendas in genetic studies of homosexuality, 1940–1994', in V. Rosario (ed) *Science and Homosexualities*, London: Routledge.

Asch, A. and Fine, M. (1988) 'Introduction: beyond pedestals', in M. Fine and A. Asch (eds) *Women with Disabilities. Essays in Psychology, Culture and Politics*, Philadelphia, PA: Temple Press.

Banat, D., Summers, S. and Pring, T. (2002) 'An investigation into carers' perceptions of the verbal comprehension ability of adults with severe learning disability', *British Journal of Learning Disability*, vol 30, pp 78–81.

Bancroft, J. (1989) *Human Sexuality and its Problems* (2nd edn), Edinburgh: Churchill Livingstone.

Barker, S., Byrne, S., Morrison, M. and Spencer, M. (2002) *Preparing for Permanency. Making Good Assessments. A Practical Resource Guide*, London: British Agencies for Fostering and Adoption.

Barnardo's (1998) *Whose Daughter Next? Children Abused Through Prostitution*, Barkingside: Barnardo's.

Barnardo's (2005) *Meeting with Respect. A Pack of Creative Ideas and Guidance for Involving Children and Young People in Meetings with Parents, Carers and Professionals*, Barkingside: Barnardo's.

Barnardo's The Junction (2005) *Safe Care Pack for Parents and Carers*, Rotherham: Barnardo's The Junction.

Barrett, D. (1997) *Child Prostitution in Britain*, London: The Children's Society.

Barter, C., Renold, E., Berridge, D. and Crawson, P. (2004) *Physical and Sexual Violence between Children in Residential Settings: Exploring Perspectives and Experiences*, Basingstoke: Palgrave Macmillan.

Bass, E. and Davis, L. (1988) *The Courage to Heal. A Guide for Women Survivors of Child Sexual Abuse*, New York, NY: Harper Collins.

Beckett, R.C. (1994) 'Cognitive behavioural treatment of sex offenders', in T. Morrison, M. Erooga and R.C. Beckett (eds) *Sexual Offending against Children: Assessment and Treatment of Male Abusers*, London: Routledge.

Bekaert, S. (2002) 'Sexual health workshops', *Paediatric Nursing*, issue 14, pp 22-5.

Bekaert, S. (2005) *Adolescents and Sex. The Handbook for Professionals Working with Young People*, Abingdon: Radcliffe Publishing Ltd.

Bennett, K.C. and Thompson, N.L. (1991) 'Accelerated ageing and homosexuality', in J.A. Lee (ed) *Gay Midlife and Maturity*, New York, NY: Harrington Press.

Bernard, C. (2001) *Constituting Lived Experience. Representations of Black Mothers in Child Sexual Abuse Discourses*, Aldershot: Ashgate.

Biehal, N., Clayden, J. and Stein, M. (1992) *Prepared for Living? A Survey of Young People Leaving the Care of Local Authorities*, London: National Children's Bureau.

Biehal, N., Clayden, J. and Stein, M. (1995) *Moving On*, London: National Children's Bureau.

Blackburn, M. (2002) *Sexuality and Disability*, Oxford: Butterworth Heinemann.

Bluett, M., Walker, A., Goodman, J. and Adeyemo, J. (2000) *Somewhere Safe: Accommodation Needs of Children and Young People at Risk on the Streets of London*, London: The Children's Society.

Bogle, J.E. and Shaul, S.S. (1981) 'Body image and the woman with a disability', in D.G. Bullard and S.E. Knight (eds) *Sexuality and Physical Disability. Personal Perspectives*, London: C.V. Mosby.

Bonvillain, N. (1995) *Women and Men: Cultural Constructions of Gender*, London: Prentice Hall.

Booth, W. and Booth, T. (1994) *Parenting under Pressure: Mothers and Fathers with Learning Difficulties*, Buckingham: Open University Press.

Booth, W. and Booth, T. (2004) 'A family at risk: multiple perspectives on parenting in child protection', *British Journal of Learning Disability*, vol 32, pp 9-15.

Branigan, T. (2004) 'Blame on the edge', *The Guardian*, 17 August.

Brecher, E. (1984) *Love, Sex and Aging: A Consumer Union Report*, Boston: Little, Brown and Co.

Brewster, S.J. (2004) 'Putting words into their mouths? Interviewing people with learning disabilities and little/no speech', *British Journal of Learning Disability*, vol 32, pp 166-9.

Brown, H.C. (1998) *Social Work and Sexuality*, London: Macmillan/ British Association of Social Workers.

Brown, H., Brammer, A., Craft, A. and McKay, C. (1996) *Towards Better Safeguards. 'Need to Know' Series. A Manual about the Sexual Abuse of Adults with Learning Disabilities*, Brighton: Pavilion Publishing.

Brown, S. (2005) *Treating Sex Offenders: An Introduction to Sex Offender Treatment Programmes*, Cullompton: Willan.

Bullock, J. and McKenzie, S. (2003) 'The menopause', in M. Jukes and M. Bollard (eds) *Contemporary Learning Disability Practice*, Salisbury: Quay Books.

Butler, J. (1990) *Gender Trouble: Feminism and the Subversion of Identity*, London: Routledge.

Calder, M.C. (ed) (2004) *Child Sexual Abuse and the Internet: Tackling the New Frontier*, Lyme Regis: Russell House Publishing.

Campbell, T.W. (2003) 'Sex offenders and actuarial risk assessments: ethical considerations', *Behavioural Sciences and the Law*, vol 21, pp 269-79.

Cann, J., Falshaw, L. and Friendship, C. (2003) *Understanding What Works: Accredited Cognitive Behavioural Skills Programmes for Adult Men and Young Offenders*, Home Office Research Findings 226, London: Home Office.

Carabine, J. (ed) (2004) *Sexualities: Personal Lives and Social Policy*, Milton Keynes/Bristol: Open University Press/The Policy Press.

Chaffin, M., Letourneau, E. and Silovsky, J.F. (2002) 'Adults, adolescents and children who sexually abuse children: a developmental perspective', in J. Myers, L. Berliner, J. Briere, C.T. Hendrix, C. Jenny and T. Reid (eds) *The APSAC Handbook on Child Maltreatment* (2nd edn), Thousand Oaks, CA: Sage Publications.

Cheek, J. (2000) *Postmodern and Poststructural Approaches to Nursing Research*, Thousand Oaks, CA: Sage Publications.

Christodoulides, T.E., Richardson, G., Graham, F., Kennedy, P.J. and Kelly, T.P. (2005) 'Risk assessment with adolescent sex offenders', *Journal of Sexual Aggression*, vol 11, pp 37-48.

Clapton, G. (2001) 'Birth fathers' lives after adoption', *Adoption and Fostering*, vol 25, pp 50-9.

Clausen, H., Kendall, M., Murray, S., Worth, A., Boyd, K. and Benton, F. (2005) 'Would palliative care patients benefit from social workers retaining the traditional "casework" role rather than working as care managers? A prospective social qualitative interview study', *British Journal of Social Work*, vol 35, pp 277-85.

Colapinto, J. (2000) *As Nature Made Him: The Boy Who was Raised as a Girl*, London: Quartet Books.

Cooke, P. and Davies, G. (2001) 'Achieving best evidence from witnesses with learning disabilities: new guidance', *British Journal of Learning Disability*, vol 29, pp 84-7.

Cooper, S. (2005) 'Understanding, treating, and managing sex offenders who deny their offence', *Journal of Sexual Aggression*, vol 11, pp 85-94.

Corbett, C., Patel, V., Erikson, M. and Friendship, C. (2003) 'The violent reconviction of sexual offenders', *Journal of Sexual Aggression*, vol 9, pp 31-40.

Corby, B. (1998) *Managing Child Sexual Abuse Cases*, London: Jessica Kingsley.

Corby, B. (2000) *Child Abuse: Towards a Knowledge Base* (2nd edn), Buckingham: Open University Press.

Corlyon, J. and McGuire, C. (1999) *Pregnancy and Parenthood: The Views and Experiences of Young People in Public Care*, London: National Children's Bureau.

Couzens, A. (1999) 'Sharing the load: group conversations with indigenous young men', in *Extending Narrative Therapy. A Collection of Practice-based Papers*, Dulwich, Australia: Dulwich Centre Publications.

Craig, L.A., Browne, K.D., Stringer, I. and Beech, A. (2005) 'Sexual recidivism: a review of static, dynamic and actuarial predictors', *Journal of Sexual Aggression*, vol 11, pp 65-84.

Craig, L. and Hutchinson, R.B. (2005) 'Sexual offenders with learning disabilities: risk, recidivism and treatment', *Journal of Sexual Aggression*, vol 11, pp 289-304.

Crain, W.C. (1985) *Theories of Development: Concepts and Applications* (2nd edn), Eaglewood Cliffs, NJ: Prentice Hall.

Curtis, H., Hoolaghan, T. and Jewitt, C. (1995) *Sexual Health Promotion in General Practice*, Oxford: Radcliffe Medical Press.

Cusik, L. (2002) 'Youth prostitution: a literature review', *Child Abuse Review*, issue 1, pp 230-51.

Cusik, S. and Martin, A. (2003) *Vulnerability and Involvement in Drug Use and Sex Work*, Home Office Research Study 268, London: Home Office.

Davies, D. (1999) 'Working with young people', in D. Davies and C. Neal (eds) *Pink Therapy. A Guide for Counsellors and Therapists Working with Lesbian, Gay and Bisexual Clients*, Buckingham: Open University Press.

Davies, D. and Neal, C. (1999a) 'An historical overview of homosexuality and therapy', in D. Davies and C. Neal (eds) *Pink Therapy. A Guide for Counsellors and Therapists Working with Lesbian, Gay and Bisexual Clients*, Buckingham: Open University Press.

Davies, D. and Neal, C. (1999b) (eds) *Pink Therapy. A Guide for Counsellors and Therapists Working with Lesbian, Gay and Bisexual Clients*, Buckingham: Open University Press.

De Shazer, S. (1988) *Clues: Investigating Solutions in Brief Therapy*, New York, NY/London: W. W. Norton.

De Shazer, S., Berg, I.K., Lipchik, E., Nunnaly, E., Molnar, A., Gingerich, W. and Weiner-Davies, M. (1986) 'Brief Therapy: Focused Solution Development', *Family Process*, vol 25, pp 207-21.

Denman, C. (2004) *Sexuality: A Biopsychosocial Approach*, Basingstoke: Palgrave Macmillan.

DfES (Department for Education and Skills) (2004a) *Responding to Allegations Against Teachers*, London, DfES.

DfES (2004b) *Safeguarding Children in Education*, London: DfES.

DH (Department of Health) (1990) *Human Fertilisation and Embryology Act 1990*, London: The Stationery Office.

DH (2001a) *Better Prevention, Better Services, Better Sexual Health: The National Strategy for Sexual Health and HIV*, London: DH.

DH (2001b) *The Children Act 1989. Guidance and Regulations. Residential Care. Vol 4*, London: HMSO.

DH (2001c) *Safeguarding Children Involved in Prostitution. Supplementary Guidance to Working Together to Safeguard Children*, London: HMSO.

DWP (Department of Work and Pensions) (2006) 'Carer's Allowance Claim Form' (www.dwp.gov.uk/advisers/claimforms/ds7001_print.pdf, accessed April 2006).

Dickman, B.J. and Roux, A.J. (2005) 'Complainants with learning disabilities in sexual abuse cases: a ten year review of a psycho-legal project in Cape Town, South Africa', *British Journal of Learning Disability*, vol 33, pp 138-44.

Dickson, S. (2004) *Sex in the City: Mapping Commercial Sex Across London*, London: Home Office/The Poppy Project.

Direct.gov.uk/Parents (2006), www.direct.gov.uk/Parents/familyIssuesAndTheLaw/ParentsRights/ParentsRightsArticles/fs/en?CONTENT_ID=4002954andchk=JsXq/k (accessed April 2006).

Dolan, Y. (1991) *Resolving Sexual Abuse. Solution-focused and Eriksonian Hypnosis for Adult Survivors*, New York, NY: W.W. Norton.

Dolan, Y. (1998) *One Small Step. Moving Beyond Trauma and Therapy to a Life of Joy*, Watsonville, CA: Papier-Mache Press.

Domenici, T. and Lesser, R.C. (1995) *Disorienting Sexuality*, New York, NY/London: Routledge.

Doolittle, M. (2004) 'Sexuality, parenthood and population: explaining fertility decline in Britain from the 1860s to 1920s', in J. Carrabine (ed) *Sexualities: Personal Lives and Social Policy*, Milton Keynes: Open University Press.

Draucker, C.B. (2000) *Counselling Survivors of Childhood Sexual Abuse*, London: Sage Publications.

Duncan, L.E. and Williams, L.M. (1998) 'Gender role socialization and male-on-male vs female-on-male child sexual abuse', *Sex Roles: A Journal of Research*, vol 39, pp 765-85.

Dunphy, R. (2000) *Sexual Politics: An Introduction*, Edinburgh: Edinburgh University Press.

Elliott, M. (1985) *Preventing Child Sexual Abuse. A Practical Guide to Talking with Children*, London: Bedford Square Press.

Erikson, E.H. (1948) *Children and Society*, Harmondsworth: Penguin.

Essex, S. (2005) Workshop presented at the International 2005 Signs of Safety Gathering, Gateshead, 26 August.

Essex, S., Gumbleton, J. and Luger, C. (1996) 'Resolutions: working with families where responsibility for sexual abuse is denied', *Child Abuse Review*, issue 5, pp 191-201.

Falshaw, L., Friendship, C., Travers, R. and Nugent, F. (2003) *Searching for 'What Works': An Evaluation of Cognitive Skills Programmes*, Home Office Research Findings 206, London: Home Office.

Farrall, S. (2004) 'Supervision, motivation and social context: what matters most when probationers desist?', in G. Mair (ed) *What Matters in Probation*, Cullompton: Willan Publishing.

Fook, J. (2002) *Social Work: Critical Theory and Practice*, Thousand Oaks, CA: Sage Publications.

Foucault, M. (1990) *The History of Sexuality: Volume 1: An Introduction* (trans. R. Hurley), New York, NY: Vintage Books.

Frank, A.O. and Maguire, G.P. (1988) *Disabling Diseases. Physical, Environmental and Psychosocial Management*, Oxford: Heinemann Medical Books.

Fraser, B. (1987) 'Sexual counselling', in G. Horobin (ed) *Sex, Gender and Care Work*, London: Jessica Kingsley.

Freeman, J., Epston, D. and Lobovits, D. (1997) *Playful Approaches to Serious Problems. Narrative Therapy with Children and their Families*, London: W.W. Norton.

Friedlander, M.L. and Stockman, S.J. (1983) 'Anchoring and Publicity Effects in Clinical Judgment', *Journal of Clinical Psychology*, vol 39, no 40, pp 637-43.

Friedrich, W. N., Fisher, J., Broughton, D., Houston, and Shafran, C.R. (1998) *Normative Sexual Behavior in Children: A contemporary sample* (www.paediatrics.org/cgi/content/full/101/4/e9, accessed 20 May 2006).

Friendship, C., Blud, L., Erikson, M. and Travers, R. (2002) *An Evaluation of Cognitive Behavioural Treatment for Prisoners*, Home Office Research Findings 161, London: Home Office.

Fu, H., Darroch, J. and Haas, T. (1999) 'Contraceptive failure rates: new estimates from the 1995 National Survey of Family Growth', *Family Planning Perspectives*, vol 31, pp 56-63.

Gilgun, J.F. (1999) 'Mapping resilience as process among adults with childhood adversities', in H.I. McCubbin, E.A. Thompson, A.I. Thompson and J.A. Futrell (eds) *The Dynamics of Resilient Families*, London: Sage Publications.

Gillies, P., Bolam, B., Johnson, S. and MacDonald, M. (2004) *A Cross Sectional Qualitative Study of the Impact of the Prostitute Outreach Workers Project in 2004*, Nottingham: Prostitutes Outreach Project/University of Nottingham.

Goddard, C.R., Saunders, B.J., Stanley, J.R. and Tucci, J. (1999) 'Structured risk assessment procedures: instruments of abuse?', *Child Abuse Review*, issue 8, pp 251-63.

Grubin, D. (1998) *Sex Offending Against Children: Understanding the Risk*, Police Research Series Paper 99, London: Home Office.

Gruskin, E.P. (1999) *Treating Lesbian and Bisexual Women. Change and Strategies for the Health Service*, London: Sage Publications.

Hackett, S. (2000) 'Sexual Aggression, Diversity and the Challenge of Anti-Oppressive Practice', *The Journal of Sexual Aggression*, vol 5, no 1, pp 4-20.

Hackett, S. (2001) *Facing the Future. A Guide for Parents of Young People who have Sexually Abused*, Lyme Regis: Russell House Publishing.

Hackett, S. (2004) *What Works for Children and Young People with Sexually Harmful Behaviours?*, Barkingside: Barnardo's.

Hackett, S., Masson, H. and Phillips, S. (2003) *Mapping and Exploring Services for Young People who have Sexually Abused Others. A Two-year Research Project funded by the Youth Justice Board, NSPCC and NOTA*, Durham: University of Durham.

Hanson, R.K. (2004) 'Sex Offender Risk Assessment', in C.R. Hollin (ed) *The Essential Handbook of Offender Assessment and Treatment.* Chichester: Wiley.

Hanson, R.K. and Bussière, M.T. (1998) 'Predicting relapse: a meta-analysis of sexual offending recidivism studies', *Journal of Consultancy and Clinical Psychology*, vol 66, pp 348-63.

Harding, C. (ed) (2001) *Sexuality: Psychoanalytic Perspectives*, Hove: Brunner Routledge.

Hargarden, H. and Llewellin, S. (1999) 'Lesbian and gay parenting issues', in D. Davies and C. Neal (eds) *Pink Therapy. A Guide for Counsellors and Therapists Working with Lesbian, Gay and Bisexual Clients*, Buckingham: Open University Press.

Harper, G. and Hopkinson, P. (2002) 'Protective behaviours: a useful approach in working with people with learning disabilities', *British Journal of Learning Disability*, vol 30, pp 149-52.

Hawkes, D., Marsh, T.I. and Wilgosh, R. (1998) *Solution Focused Therapy. A Handbook for Health Care Professionals*, Oxford: Butterworth Heinemann.

Health Education Authority (1998) *Unintended Teenage Conceptions*, London: Health Education Authority.

Hearn, J. and Ford, D. (1991) *Studying Men and Masculinity: A Sourcebook of Literature and Materials*, Bradford: University of Bradford.

Hicks, S. (2003) 'The Christian right and homophobic discourse: a response to "evidence" that lesbian and gay parenting damages children', *Sociological Research Online*, vol 8, no 4 (www.socresonline.org.uk/8/4/hicks.html).

Hicks, S. (2005a) 'Sexualities: social work theories and practice', in R. Adams, L. Dominelli and M. Payne (eds) *Social Work Futures: Crossing Boundaries, Transforming Practice*, Basingstoke: Palgrave Macmillan.

Hicks, S. (2005b) 'Genealogy's desire: practices of kinship amongst lesbian and gay foster carers and adopters', *British Journal of Social Work*, vol 36, no 5, pp 761-76.

Hicks, S. and McDermott, J. (1999) 'Editorial essay', in S. Hicks and J. McDermott (eds) *Lesbian and Gay Fostering and Adoption. Extraordinary yet Ordinary*, London: Jessica Kingsley.

Home Office (2005) *Tackling Sexual Violence. Guidance to Local Partnerships*, London: Home Office.

Home Office (2006a) *Convicting Rapists and Protecting Victims – Justice for Victims of Rape*, London: Home Office.

Home Office (2006b) *A Coordinated Prostitution Strategy and a Summary of Responses to 'Paying the Price'*, London: Home Office.

Home Office (2006c) *Consultation on the Possession of Extreme Pornographic Material: Summary of Responses and Next Steps*, London: Home Office.

Hood-Williams, J. (1996) 'Goodbye to sex and gender', *Sociological Review*, vol 44, no 1, pp 1-16.

Hooker, J. and Wallace, B. (2000) 'Sexual health for sale', in H. Wilson and S. McAndrew (eds) *Sexual Health. Foundations for Practice*, London: Balliere Tindall (in association with the Royal College of Nursing).

hooks, b. (1996) 'Continued devaluation of black womanhood', in S. Jackson and S. Scott (eds) *Feminism and Sexuality: A Reader*, Edinburgh: Edinburgh University Press.

Houston, S. and Griffiths, H. (2000) 'Reflections on risk in child protection: is it time for a shift in paradigms?', *Child and Family Social Work*, vol 5, pp 1-10.

Hughes, B. (2000) *Older People and Community Care. Critical Theory and Practice*, Buckingham: Open University Press.

Itzin, C. (2005) 'Victims of violence and abuse prevention programme on health and mental health', in *Improving Outcomes for Victims of Sexual Violence. A Strategic Partnership Approach. Conference Report*, London: Home Office/Department of Health/Crown Prosecution Service/Association of Chief Police Officers.

Iveson, C. (1990) *Whose Life? Community Care of Older People and their Families*, London: B.T. Press.

Jackson, S. and Scott, S. (eds) (1996) *Feminism and Sexuality: A Reader*, Edinburgh: Edinburgh University Press.

Jeffreys, S. (1996) 'Heterosexuality and the desire for gender', in D. Richardson (ed) *Theorising Heterosexuality*, Buckingham: Open University Press.

Jenkins, A. (1990) *Invitations to Responsibility*, Adelaide: Dulwich Centre Publications.

Jones, D.P.H. and Ramchandani, P. (1999) *Child Sexual Abuse. Informing Practice from Research*, Oxford: Radcliffe Medical Press.

Katz, J. (1990) 'The invention of heterosexuality', *Socialist Review*, vol 20, pp 7-34.

Kelly, L. (1996) 'Weasel words: paedophiles and the cycle of abuse', *Trouble and Strife*, issue 33, pp 44-9.

Kelly, L., Wingfield, R., Burton, S. and Regan, L. (1995) *Splintered Lives: Sexual Exploitation of Children in the Context of Children's Rights and Child Protection*, Ilford/London: Barnardo's/Child Abuse and Woman Abuse Studies Unit, University of North London.

Kenen, S. (1997) 'Who counts when you're counting homosexuals? Hormones and homosexuality in mid-twentieth century America', in V. Rosario (ed) *Science and Homosexualities*, London: Routledge.

Kinsey, A.C., Pomeroy, W.B. and Martin, C.E. (1948) *Sexual Behaviour in the Human Male*, Philadelphia, PA/London: W.B. Saunders.

Kitzinger, C. and Wilkinson, S. (1993) (eds) *Heterosexuality: A Feminism and Psychology Reader*, London: Sage Publications.

Kline, P. (1972) *Fact and Fantasy in Freudian Theory*, London: Methuen.

Knight, S.E. (1981) 'Introduction', in D.G. Bullard and S.E. Knight (eds) *Sexuality and Physical Disability. Personal Perspectives*, London: C.V. Mosby.

Lambert, M.J. and Ogles, B.M. (2004) 'The efficacy and effectiveness of psychotherapy', in S.L. Bergen and A.E. Garfield (eds) *Handbook of Psychotherapy and Behaviour Change*, New York, NY: Wiley.

Lancaster, R.N. and di Leonardo, M. (1997) *The Gender Sexuality Reader*, London: Routledge.

Lasker, J.N. and Borg, S. (1994) *In Search of Parenthood. Coping with Infertility and High-Tech Conception* (revised edn), Philadelphia, PA: Temple Press.

Leichtentritt, R.D. and Arad, B.D. (2005) 'Young male street workers' life histories and current experiences', *British Journal of Social Work*, vol 35, pp 483-509.

Lenihan, T. and Dean, P. (2000) 'Child prostitution in England', in D. Barrett (ed) with E. Barret and N. Mullenger, *Youth Prostitution in the New Europe*, Lyme Regis: Russell House Publishing.

Lenz, R. and Chaves, B. (1981) 'Becoming active partners', in D.G. Bullard and S.E. Knight (eds) *Sexuality and Physical Disability. Personal Perspectives*, London: C.V. Mosby.

Letellier, P. (1999) 'Rape', in B. Leventhal and S.E. Lundy (eds) *Same-Sex Domestic Violence. Strategies for Change*, London: Sage Publications.

LeVay, S. (1993) *The Sexual Brain*, Cambridge, MA: Massachusetts Institute of Technology Press.

LeVay, S. (1996) *Queer Science: The Uses and Abuses of Research into Homosexuality*, Cambridge, MA: Massachusetts Institute of Technology Press.

Lewis, E. (1976) 'The management of stillbirth – coping with an unreality', *Lancet*, issue 2, pp 619-20.

Lindsay, J. (2001) *Providing Sexual Health to Teenagers*, London: North and South Islington Primary Care Trust.

Long, K. and Holmes, N. (2001) 'Helping adults with a learning disability keep safe in the local community: a report of a group design, development and evaluation', *British Journal of Learning Disability*, vol 29, pp 139-44.

Mack, S. and Tucker, J. (1996) *Fertility Counselling*, London: Balliere Tindall (in association with the Royal College of Nursing).

Mair, G. (2004) 'The origins of what works in England and Wales: a house built on sand?', in G. Mair (ed) *What Matters in Probation*, Cullompton: Willan Publishing.

Mallon, G.P. (1999) *Let's Get This Straight: A Gay- and Lesbian-affirming Approach to Child Welfare*, New York, NY: Columbia University Press.

Mason, M.-C. (1993) *Male Infertility. Men Talking*, London: Routledge.

Masson, J.M. (1984) *The Assault on Truth: Freud's Suppression of the Seduction Theory*, New York, NY: Farrar, Straus and Giroux.

May, T., Edmunds, M. and Hough, M. with Harvey, C. (1999) *The Street Business: The Links between Sex and Drug Markets*, Police Research Services Papers 118, London: Home Office.

Mayes, G.M., Currie, E.F., Macleod, L., Gillies, J.B. and Warden, D.A. (1992) *Child Sexual Abuse. A Review of Literature and Educational Materials*, Edinburgh: Scottish Academic Press.

McCarthy, M. and Millard, L. (2003) 'Discussing the menopause with women with learning disabilities', *British Journal of Learning Disability*, vol 31, pp 9-17.

Medina, J.J. (1996) *The Clock of Ages. Why we Age, How we Age, Winding Back the Clock*, Cambridge: Cambridge University Press.

Merrill, G.S. (1999) '1 in 3 and 1 in 10: sexual and dating violence prevention groups for lesbian, gay, bisexual and transgendered youth', in B. Leventhal and S.E. Lundy (eds) *Same-Sex Domestic Violence. Strategies for Change*, London: Sage Publications.

Middleton, L. (1999) *Disabled Children: Challenging Social Exclusion*, Oxford: Blackwell Science.

Milner, J. (1986) *Social Work and Sexual Problems*, Birmingham: Pepar.

Milner, J. (2001) *Women and Social Work. Narrative Approaches*, Basingstoke: Palgrave Macmillan.

Milner, J. (2003) 'Narrative group work with young women – and their mobile phones', *International Journal of Narrative Therapy and Community Work*, issue 3, pp 54-60.

Milner, J. (2004a) 'From "disappearing" to "demonised": the effects on men and women of professional interventions based on challenging men who are violent', *Critical Social Policy*, vol 24, pp 79-101.

Milner, J. (2004b) 'Groupwork with young women', *Context*, issue 74, pp 14-17.

Milner, J. and Blyth, E. (1989) *Coping with Child Sexual Abuse; A Guide for Teachers*, London: Longman.

Milner, J. and Myers, S. (2007) *Working with Violence: Practices and Policies in Risk Assessment and Management*, Basingstoke: Palgrave Macmillan.

Milner, J. and O'Byrne, P. (2002) *Assessment in Social Work* (2nd edn), Basingstoke: Palgrave Macmillan.

Milner, J., Jessop, D., Lofthouse, N., Kaur, J. and Deo, S. (2002) *Young People Involved in Prostitution Related to Drug Use in Ravensthorpe*, Mirfield: Northorpe Hall Child and Family Trust.

Murray Parkes, C. (1986) *Bereavement. Studies of Grief in Adult Life*, London: Penguin.

Myers, S. (2002) 'Language, discourse and empowerment: changing approaches to children and young people who have sexually abused others', *Children and Society*, vol 16, pp 334-45.

Myers, S. with McLaughlin, M. and Warwick, K. (2003) 'The day the Touching Monster came: narrative and solution focused approaches to working with children and young people with sexually inappropriate behaviour', *Journal of Educational Psychology*, vol 20, pp 76-89.

Nash, M. (1999) *Police, Probation and Protecting the Public*, London: Blackstone Press.

National Probation Directorate (2002) *The Treatment and Risk Management of Sexual Offenders in Custody and in the Community*, London: HMSO.

National Probation Directorate (2004) *Sex Offender Strategy for the National Probation Service*, London: HMSO.

Nelkin, D. and Lindee, S. (1995) 'The media-ted gene: stories of gender and race', in J. Terry and J. Urla (eds) *Deviant Bodies: Critical Perspectives on Difference in Science and Popular Culture*, Bloomington, IN: Indiana University Press.

Nichols, K. (2003) *Psychological Care of Ill People and Injured People. A Clinical Guide*, Maidenhead: Open University Press.

Nusbaum, M. and Rosenfeld, J.A. (2004) *Sexual Health Across the Lifecycle. A Practical Guide for Clinicians*, Cambridge: Cambridge University Press.

Nye, R.A. (1999) *Sexuality: A Reader*, Oxford: Oxford University Press.

Nylund, D. (2000) *Treating Huckleberry Finn: A New Narrative Approach to Working with Kids Diagnosed ADD/ADHD*, San Francisco, CA: Jossey Bass.

Oakley, A. (1972) *Sex, Gender and Society*, London: Maurice Temple Smith.

O'Brien, C. (1999) 'Contested Territory: Sexualities and Social Work', in A.S. Chambon, A. Irving and L. Epstein (eds) *Reading Foucault for Social Work*. New York: Columbia University Press.

O'Callaghan, A.C., Murphy, G. and Clare, I.C.H. (2003) 'The impact of abuse on men and women with severe learning disabilities and their families', *British Journal of Learning Disability*, vol 3, pp 175-80.

O'Donnell, K. (1999) 'Lesbian and gay families: legal perspectives', in G. Jagger and C. Wright (eds) *Changing Family Values*, London: Routledge.

Orlinsky, D.E., Ronnestad, M.H. and Willutzki, U. (2004) 'Fifty years of psychotherapy process–outcome research', in S.L. Bergen and A.E. Garfield (eds) *Handbook of Psychotherapy and Behaviour Change*, New York, NY: Wiley.

Osterhuis, M., Solomon, F. and Green, M. (1984) *Bereavement, Consequences and Care*, Washington, DC: National Academy Press.

Owen, M. (1999a) *Novices, Old Hands and Professionals: Adoption by Single People*, London: British Agencies for Fostering and Adoption.

Owen, M. (1999b) 'Single adopters and sibling groups', in A. Mullender (ed) *We Are Family. Sibling Relationships in Placement and Beyond*, London: British Agencies for Fostering and Adoption.

Palmore, E. (1982) 'Predictors of the longevity difference: a 25 year follow-up', *Gerontologist*, vol 22, pp 513-18.

Parmar, A., Sampson, A. and Diamond, A. (2005) *Tackling Domestic Violence. Providing Support to Survivors from Black Minority Ethnic Communities*, London: Home Office.

Parsons, T. (1999) 'Normal female anatomy, physiology, and behaviour', in J. Tomlinson (ed) *ABC of Sexual Health*, London: BMJ Books.

Parton, N. and O'Byrne, P. (2000) *Constructive Social Work*, Basingstoke: Macmillan.

Pearce, J. and Smith, R. (2003) 'Rebels without a clause', *Community Care*, issue 12, June, pp 34-5.

Pearce, J.J., Williams, M. and Galvin, C. (2002) *It's Someone Taking Part of You. A Study of Young Women and Sexual Exploitation*, London: National Children's Bureau/Joseph Rowntree Foundation/Midddlesex University/National Society for the Prevention of Cruelty to Children.

Percival, J. and Hanson, J. (2005) '"I'm like a tree a million miles from the water's edge": social care and inclusion of the older people with visual impairment', *British Journal of Social Work*, vol 35, pp 189-205.

Plummer, K. (1975) *Sexual Stigma: An Interactionist Account*, London: Routledge and Kegan Paul.

Plummer, K. (1984) 'Sexual diversity: a sociological perspective', in K. Howells (ed) *Sexual Diversity*, Oxford: Blackwell.

Polaschek, D.L.L. (2001) 'Relapse prevention: offense process models and the treatment of sexual offenders', *Journal of Interpersonal Violence*, vol 6, pp 523-44.

POW (Prostitute Outreach Workers) (2004) *Prostitute Outreach Workers Annual Report 2004*, Nottingham: POW.

Puglia, L., Stough, C., Carter, J.D. and Joseph, M. (2005) 'The emotional intelligence of adult sex offenders: ability based EI assessment', *Journal of Sexual Aggression*, vol 11, pp 249-58.

Quillam, S. (2005) '"Teen mags": helpful or harmful?', *Journal of Family Planning and Reproductive Health Care*, vol 31, no 1, pp 77-9.

Ratigan, B. (1999) 'Working with gay older men', in D. Davies and C. Neal (eds) *Pink Therapy. A Guide for Counsellors and Therapists Working with Lesbian, Gay and Bisexual Clients*, Buckingham: Open University Press.

Read, J. (1999) 'Sexual problems associated with infertility, pregnancy and ageing', in J. Tomlinson (ed) *ABC of Sexual Health*, London: BMJ Books.

Refugee Council/Department of Health (2006) *Caring for Dispersed Asylum Seekers* (www.asylumaid.org.uk).

Refugee Women's Resource Project/Asylum Aid (2005) *Lip Service or Implementation? The Home Office Gender Guidance and Women's Asylum Claims in the UK*, London: Asylum Aid.

Richards, S., Steel, M. and Singer, D. (2006) *Hope Betrayed: An Analysis of Women Victims of Trafficking and their Claims of Asylum*, London: Eaves Poppy Project/Asylum Aid.

Richardson, D. (ed) (1996) *Theorising Heterosexuality*, Milton Keynes: Open University Press.

Richardson, G. (2005) 'Early maladaptive schemas in a sample of British adolescent sexual abusers: implications for therapy', *Journal of Sexual Aggression*, vol 11, pp 259-76.

Rousso, H. (1988) 'Daughters with disabilities: deficient women or minority women?', in M. Fine and A. Asch (eds) *Women with Disabilities. Essays in Psychology, Culture and Politics*, Philadelphia, PA: Temple Press.

Ruse, M. (1988) *Homosexuality: A Philosophical Inquiry*, Oxford: Basil Blackwell.

Rutter, M. (1999) 'Resilience concepts and findings: implications for family therapy', *Journal of Family Therapy*, vol 21, pp 119-44.

Said, E. (2003) *Orientalism: Western Conceptions of the Orient*, London: Penguin.

Saradjian, J. (1996) *Women who Sexually Abuse Children: From Research to Clinical Practice*, Chichester: Wiley.

Saraga, E. (ed) (1998) *Embodying the Social: Constructions of Difference*, London/Milton Keynes: Routledge/Open University Press.

Scourfield, J. (2003) *Gender and Child Protection*, Basingstoke: Palgrave Macmillan.

Scruton, R. (1986) *Sexual Desire*, London: Weidenfeld and Nicolson.

Seal, A. (2004) 'Taking care. Helping children learn to keep themselves safer', in V. White and J. Harris (eds) *Developing Good Practice in Children's Services*, London: Jessica Kingsley.

Seidman, S. (1994) 'Queer-ing sociology, sociologising queer theory: an introduction', *Sociological Theory*, vol 12, pp 166-79.

Selekman, M.D. (2002) *Living on the Razor's Edge. Solution-oriented Brief Family Therapy with Self-harming Adolescents*, New York, NY/London: W.W. Norton.

SEU (Social Exclusion Unit) (1999) *Teenage Pregnancy Strategy*, London: HMSO.

Shakespeare, T., Gillespie-Sells, K. and Davies, D. (1996) *The Sexual Politics of Disability: Untold Desires*, London: Cassell.

Sharpe, H. (2001) *Just Gateways? Towards a Changed Police Response to People with Learning Difficulties as Victims of Crime*, London: Values into Action.

Shildrick, M. (2004) 'Silencing sexuality: the regulation of the disabled body', in J. Carabine (ed) *Sexualities: Personal Lives and Social Policy*, Milton Keynes: Open University Press.

Silcock, L. (2003) *Occupational Therapy and Multiple Sclerosis*, London: Whurr Publishers.

Silver, E. and Miller, L.L. (2002) 'A cautionary note on the use of actuarial risk assessment tools for social control', *Crime and Delinquency*, vol 8, pp 138-61.

Sinclair, I. and Gibbs, I. (1998) *Children's Homes: A Study in Diversity*, Chichester: Wiley.

Sinclair, R., Garrett, L. and Berridge, D. (1995) *Social Work and Assessment with Adolescents*, London: National Children's Bureau.

Skeggs, B. (1997) *Formations of Class and Gender: Becoming Respectable*, London: Sage Publications.

Skidmore, P. (2000) *Researching Youth Prostitution*, London: Guildhall University.

Smith, A.M. (1994) *New Right Discourse on Race and Sexuality*, Cambridge: Cambridge University Press.

Socriades, C.W. (1978) *Homosexuality*, New York, NY: Jason Aranson.

Soothill, K., Francis, B., Sanderson, B. and Acklery, E. (2000) 'Sex offenders: specialists, generalists or both?', *British Journal of Criminology*, vol 40, pp 56-67.

Squire, A. (2002) *Health and Well-being for Older People. Foundations for Practice*, London: Balliere Tindall.

Stoler, A.L. (1995) *Race and the Education of Desire: Foucault's History of Sexuality and the Colonial Order of Things*, Durham, NC/London: Duke University Press.

Sullivan, M. (2005) 'Help for men who have been sexually assaulted. Understanding male sexual assault', in *Improving Outcomes for Victims of Sexual Violence. A Strategic Partnership Approach. Conference Report*, London: Home Office/Department of Health/Crown Prosecution Service/Association of Chief Police Officers.

Swain, J., French, S. and Cameron, C. (2003) *Controversial Issues in a Disability Society*, Buckingham: Open University Press.

Swann, S. (1998) 'A model for understanding abuse through prostitution and Barnardo's Streets and Lanes Project', in *Whose Daughter Next? Children Abused through Prostitution*, Ilford: Barnardo's.

Swigar, M.E., Bowers, M.B. and Flecks, S. (1976) 'Grieving and unplanned pregnancy', *Psychiatry*, vol 39, pp 72-9.

Taylor, T. (1997) *The Prehistory of Sex*, London: Fourth Estate.

Terry, P. (1997) *Counselling the Elderly and their Carers*, Basingstoke: Macmillan.

Thomas, C. (1999) *Female Forms. Experiencing and Understanding Disability*, Buckingham: Open University Press.

Thomas, T. (2005) *Sex Crime: Sex Offending and Society* (2nd edn), Cullompton: Willan.

Thompson, N. (1993) *Anti-Discriminatory Practice*, Basingstoke: Palgrave Macmillan.

Tomlinson, J. (1999) 'Normal male anatomy, physiology, and behaviour', in J. Tomlinson (ed) *ABC of Sexual Health*, London: BMJ Books.

Tudway, J.A. and Darmoody, M. (2005) 'Clinical assessment of adult sexual offenders with learning difficulties', *Journal of Sexual Aggression*, vol 11, pp 277-88.

Turnell, A. and Edwards, S. (1999) *Signs of Safety: A Solution and Safety Oriented Approach to Child Protection Casework*, New York, NY/London: W.W. Norton.

Vivian-Byrne, S.E. (2002) 'Using context and difference in sex offender treatment: an integrated approach', *Journal of Sexual Aggression*, vol 8, pp 59-73.

Walker, A., Kershaw, C. and Nicolas, S. (2006) *Crime in England and Wales. Home Office Statistical Bulletin 12/06*, London: HMSO.

Walker, Z., Townsend, J.L., Bell, J. and Marshall, S. (1999) 'An opportunity for teenage health promotion in general practice: an assessment of current provision and needs', *Health Education Journal*, vol 58, pp 218-27.

Walsh, F. (1999) 'Partner abuse', in D. Davies and C. Neal (eds) *Pink Therapy. A Guide for Counsellors and Therapists Working with Lesbian, Gay and Bisexual Clients*, Buckingham: Open University Press.

Ward, M. and Wolverton, M. (1990) 'Risk assessment: the emperor's new clothes?', *Child Welfare*, vol 69, pp 483-511.

Weeks, J. (1985) *Sexuality and its Discontents: Meanings, Myths and Modern Sexualities*, London: Routledge and Kegan Paul.

Weeks, J. (1989) *Sex, Politics and Society: The Regulation of Sexuality*, Harlow: Longman.

Weeks, J. (2003) *Sexuality* (2nd edn), London: Routledge.

Weinberg, G. (1972) *Society and the Healthy Homosexual*, Garden City, NY: Doubleday Anchor.

Wellings, K., Field, J., Johnson, N. and Wadsworth, J. (1994) *Sexual Behaviour in Britain. The National Survey of Sexual Attitudes and Lifestyles*, London: Penguin Books.

White, M. and Epston, D. (1990) *Narrative Means to Therapeutic Ends*, New York, NY: W.W. Norton.

Wilson, E.O. (1975) *Sociobiology: The New Synthesis*, Cambridge, MS and London: Cambridge University Press.

Wilton, T. (2000) *Sexualities in Health and Social Care. A Textbook*, Buckingham: Open University Press.

Wilton, T. (2004) *Sexual (Dis)Orientation: Gender, Sex, Desire and Self-Fashioning*, Basingstoke: Palgrave Macmillan.

Witney, C. (2004) 'Original fathers. An exploration into the experiences of birth fathers involved in adoption in the mid twentieth century', *Adoption and Fostering*, vol 28, pp 52-61.

Wittgenstein, L. (1963) *Philosophical Investigations* (3rd edn), Oxford: Blackwell.

Wittig, M. (1992) *The Straight Mind and Other Essays*, London: Harvester Wheatsheaf.

Women and Equality Unit (2005) www.womenandequalityunit.gov.uk/civilpartnership/cpguide2005.pdf (accessed April 2005).

Worling, J.R. and Curwen, T. (2000) 'Adolescent sexual offender recidivism: success of specialised treatment and implications for risk prediction', *Child Abuse and Neglect*, issue 24, pp 965-82.

Wright, J. (2003) 'Considering issues of domestic violence and abuse in palliative care and bereavement situations', *International Journal of Narrative Therapy and Community Work*, issue 3, pp 72-7.

Young, V. (1999) 'Working with older lesbians', in D. Davies and C. Neal (eds) *Pink Therapy. A Guide for Counsellors and Therapists Working with Lesbian, Gay and Bisexual Clients*, Buckingham: Open University Press.

Index